Terence Whitaker was born near Barnsley and was educated in Lancashire and Yorkshire. He spent nine years in the Merchant Navy, travelling the world on board oil tankers. After two years in the prison service, he joined the Ministry of Labour - now the Manpower Services Commission — where he has worked ever since. Mr Whitaker is married with one daughter.

He has written a play for disabled people to perform in wheelchairs, *He'll Have to Go, Mrs Lovejoy,* and a book similar to this one entitled *Lancashire's Ghosts and Legends*.

By the same author

Lancashire's Ghosts and Legends

TERENCE W. WHITAKER

Yorkshire's Ghosts and Legends

GRANADA
London Toronto Sydney New York

Published by Granada Publishing Limited in 1983

ISBN 0 583 13592 7

A Granada Paperback Original
Copyright © Terence W. Whitaker 1983

Granada Publishing Limited
Frogmore, St Albans, Herts AL2 2NF
and
36 Golden Square, London W1R 4AH
515 Madison Avenue, New York, NY 10022, USA
117 York Street, Sydney, NSW 2000, Australia
100 Skyway Avenue, Rexdale, Ontario, M9W 3A6, Canada
61 Beach Road, Auckland, New Zealand

Printed and bound in Great Britain by
Cox & Wyman Ltd, Reading
Set in Times

Granada ®
Granada Publishing ®

For
Marjorie and Julia
With love.

Acknowledgements

Photographs were supplied and are reproduced by kind permission of the following:
BBC Radio Sheffield 1; Marjorie Whitaker 3; Albert Paradise 7; Halifax *Evening Courier* 8; Michael Joseph 20; all the others are the property of the author.

Contents

Foreword

by Gerald Main, BBC Radio Lancashire.

Morbid and eccentric . . . that is how I thought Terence Whitaker would turn out to be when I went to interview him about his first book *Lancashire's Ghosts and Legends*. I therefore approached the assignment with more than a little trepidation and scepticism, but much to my relief, I found the author to be a warm and jovial Yorkshireman with a fine sense of humour.

I was fortunate enough to persuade Terry to take part in a series of radio programmes entitled 'Ghosthunt'. After six weeks of frantically chasing phantoms which I still didn't really believe were there, we encountered the ghost of Lancashire's famous Chingle Hall — and seeing is believing.

Although you should never believe everything you read or hear, I'm sure this book will at least go a long way in persuading even the most sceptical to keep an open mind on this fascinating subject.

Blackburn 1981.

Preface

Following an appeal to newspapers for real ghost stories to research this book, I received a letter from a gentleman who posed the question . . . 'Real ghost stories? How can there be real ghost stories, when there are no real ghosts?'

But are there no real ghosts? The reader might never have seen one, but it does not necessarily follow that they do not exist. Man knows a great deal about his immediate environment, but there is a vast area on the misty boundaries of this life of which he knows very little. The supernatural apparition can appear very normal indeed, both in its appearance and in the sound it makes: that girl in the tight-fitting denim trousers, the old man coming out of the bookie's shop, the dirty faced child waiting to cross the road — you have never seen them before. You might never see them again. They are the images which impinge on your conscious for a moment of time and are then forgotten. They could in fact be ghosts, just waiting to be seen by those who have eyes to see.

I believe we all enjoy a good ghost story. Even the most hardened sceptic will enjoy a tale of the supernatural, of inexplicable sounds and smells, of ghostly figures in the night hours. We all like to be scared, provided we are in the company of others and in warm convivial surroundings. For although we have a reputation for being dour, we Yorkshire folk are not above a quiet belief in the existence of the supernatural.

The term 'ghost' describes an astonishing variety of apparitions, from the misty white figure drifting through a lonely graveyard, to balls of light or fire, smelling of sulphur, which have been reported·on the sites of ancient battlefields. There are the ghosts of vengeful monks and weeping girls, of horses, dogs and birds, of coaches and even aircraft. There are headless ghosts, legless ghosts and invisible ghosts that can drag the living out of bed or cause blood to be seen to ooze out of the floorboards. There are even sexy ghosts.

Then there are the ghosts that announce their presence by whistling and moaning, by footsteps, or the touch of a clammy hand on the victim's skin. Kindly ghosts, cruel ghosts and ghosts of the living, as well as the dead.

However, for the purpose of this book, this great nether-world of Yorkshire ghosts can conveniently be divided into two groups: traditional and legendary phantoms, such as those at Burton Agnes Hall or Spofforth Castle, which almost everyone has heard of, but very few can actually claim to have seen: and the more ordinary, and to my mind interesting spectres, which have been vouched for by many witnesses, but whose appearances are all too often un-explained.

Whether the reader is a believer in the supernatural or a hardened sceptic, I hope these stories will help you think along the lines that not all supernatural phenomena are figments of the imagination. Many of the stories in this book are the first-hand experiences of people I have met or who have written to tell me of the apparitions they have to live with in their daily lives. A number of these stories have never been in print before; others are about to have an-other airing. I have not set out with the deliberate intention of trying to terrify my readers, there are other authors far better qualified to do that than I am. Nor have I tried to answer many of the questions which surround these ghosts and poltergeists. In the main I have recorded the para-normal experiences as they were related to me by a vast number of honest and intelligent Yorkshire folk.

The other stories in this book go back, in some cases, into the mists of time. They are tales which have been told around countless firesides for centuries and handed down from one generation to the next, helping to satisfy man's basic need for a story. They may have become distorted in the re-telling, but they will have retained some of their original elements and have certainly lost none of their appeal today.

A great many people have helped me to write this book. To these people I owe a great personal debt and offer my sincere thanks for their assistance. There are some people who deserve a special mention; my wife Marjorie and daughter Julia, for their help, patience and encouragement; my good friend Gerald Main, of BBC Radio Lancashire, who produces my radio series 'Ghosthunt' and who kindly consented to write the foreword to this volume; Ralph Robinson and Clive Lawrence of BBC Radio Sheffield; Caroline Woodruff, BBC Radio Manchester; Mr Michael Joseph, City Varieties Music Hall, Leeds; Mr F.E. Hurrell, Editor, *Darlington and Stockton Times*; Mr Gregor MacGregor, The Georgian Theatre, Richmond; my ever helpful friends at Burnley Central Library; the staff at York Central Library; the many editors of newspapers and magazines throughout Yorkshire, who very kindly inserted my letters asking for ghost stories; the many contributors, who for a variety of reasons wish to remain anonymous; and the following citizens of Yorkshire who kindly consented to my mentioning their names and without whom this book could never have been written:
Mr M. Atkins, Whitby; Mr M. Atkins, Chesterfield; Mrs M. Auty, Rastrick; Miss J. Bailey, Rotherham; Mr S. Bennedick, *Yorkshire Post* Newspapers; Mrs D. Bennett, Leeds; Mr and Mrs F. Berridge, Halifax; Mrs B. Bould, Wakefield; Mr. J.H. Bradey, Sheffield; Mrs D. Branks, Barnsley; Mr M. Bryant, Halifax; Mrs Claytor, Sheffield;

Mrs E. Dacre, Wakefield; Mrs M. Dannott, Huddersfield; Mr T. Dignam, Sheffield; Mrs R. Dixon, Dewsbury; Mrs I. Elliott, Sheffield; Mr W. Foggitt, Thirsk; Mrs M. Hall, Huddersfield; Mrs J. Halstead, Sowerby Bridge; Mr J. Harris, Halifax; Mrs H. Jessop, Liversedge; Mr W. Jordan, Halifax; Mr J.C. Kenyon, Harrogate; Mrs P. Kitchen, Mirfield; Mr Kitching, Horsforth; Mrs J.M. Kitson, Huddersfield; Mr N. Lancaster, Huddersfield; Mrs A. Lathom, Batley; Mr P. Lawton, Huddersfield; Mr W.D. Mather, Sheffield; Mrs F. Mills, Denaby Main; Mr A. Paradise, Stainland; Mrs E. Parker, Brighouse; Mrs Parrott, Sowerby Bridge; Mr J. Patrick, Salisbury, Wilts.; Mr C.R. Pocklington, Mexborough; Mrs Roberts, Sheffield; Mr C. Robinson, Halifax; Mrs G. Robinson, Market Weighton; Colin and Jane Rushworth, Weaver's Restaurant, Haworth; Mrs J. Shackleton, Huddersfield; Mr A.H. Sproat, Harrogate; Mrs C. Sykes, Huddersfield; Mrs A.K. Vaughan-Morris, Featherstone; Mrs D. Welsh, Wakefield; Ronald and Joyce Whitaker, Crown Hotel, Selby; Mr B. Wildsmith, Birstall; Mrs B. Yates, Hull.

To all these lovely people this book is humbly dedicated, with grateful thanks.

Burnley 1981

These nightly shadows pale,
Haunt only remembered places,
The long forgotten memories of an age
Come forth for only those with eyes to see.

Julia Whitaker

CHAPTER 1

Spectral Workmates

A broadcasting studio would, one might think, be the last place where one might meet a ghost. Not so, for the studios of BBC Radio Sheffield, built over a hundred years ago for a prominent citizen of the city, have a history which is beyond explanation, for amongst the modern, sophisticated equipment and the non-stop working atmosphere of today, something or somebody lingers.

I am indebted to Ralph Robinson, senior producer of BBC Radio Sheffield for allowing me to quote his article in the *Radio Sheffield Magazine*.

Says Ralph, 'It is one of the standing jokes of the station that the ghost may be somebody who was separated from a visiting party and expired whilst trying to find the way out.'

The building in Westbourne Road has a pleasant, rambling quality that can flummox many a first-time visitor. By day it can be eerie enough, but at night, with the wind rustling through the trees and the occasional owl hooting eerily in the branches, Ralph says, 'It can make Dracula's castle look like a Wendy house.'

Whoever or whatever the ghost might be, it is not a malevolent presence. Two people have claimed to have seen something, whilst others have heard it or sensed it. One young lady, who lives in Derbyshire, spent a late evening in Sheffield and had to get up very early in the morning to do an early shift at the studios. Instead of going home, she bedded down at the radio station but an hour later she got up and drove home because she felt she was not alone.

Ralph himself says that he has walked out three times

late at night: once because strange things were happening to signal lights on electronic equipment and twice because he felt he was being watched.

A freelance reporter, Richard Hemmingway, was entirely on his own in the newsroom when he heard the front door open and footsteps go through the hall and up the stairs. He went to see who it was and found himself alone. Later he heard lights being switched on and off.

Not only is the presence felt late at night. One Sunday afternoon, engineer Peter Mason noticed that a recorded programme which was being broadcast had become barely audible. He hurried to the studio and found that a volume control knob on the main control panel had been turned down. No one had been in the studio and when he tried to reproduce the fault, he failed.

Two people, Gerry Kersey, BBC Radio Sheffield theatre critic, and Phil Baldy, former sports producer and reporter, have been closest to the ghost.

Gerry Kersey often works into the small hours and has become used to the clicks and bumps in other parts of the station, but one night he was really scared. He was passing a cupboard, when the door suddenly sprang open and tape spools started to come out, one at a time, as if being thrown. Gerry thought someone was having a joke at his expense. He flung the door wide open and was amazed to find no one there. On another occasion he was alone in the building at 2 A.M. and while editing a tape, he happened to glance up at the studio door. There is a square port-hole in every such door at the radio station and Gerry swears he saw a shadow pass across it. He went out and called, but there was no one there.

Phil Baldy had the closest encounter of all one night in August 1978. Having finished the late news shift and feeling tired, he went to the door of the newsroom, which looks out on to the main stairway and an archway. At that moment, something white fluttered across the archway. It was no particular shape, just a white form, but there was no way in which Phil was going to investigate.

Shaken, he switched out all the lights; the last at the glass-panelled front door. The switch is four or five yards from the door and, having switched off, one has to grope for the door latch in the dark. Phil was unable to find the latch. He fumbled frantically in the dark while panic mounted. Finally he got the door open and with a sigh of relief, closed it behind him and turned to double lock it from the outside. The glass panels of the door reflected the yellow street lights in Westbourne Road behind him. He could see his reflection . . . except that the face he saw was not his. Needless to say, he fled.

Ralph said that when Phil told him the story the following day, he said that the face he saw was that of an old man. Phil was a young man!

The premises of the firm of Air Heating Limited, of Yeadon near Leeds, are subject to paranormal phenomena usually ascribed to poltergeist activities. The incidents were first reported in 1970, having been occurring over a period of eight or nine months.

The building, according to the records, was originally constructed as a church in 1834 and later it became a church school. At the turn of the century, a brewer's dray ran out of control and collided with the building. The driver was thrown through a window and died instantly. This could possibly be the cause of the present phenomena but more likely is the fact that during the Second World War, when the building was turned over to industry and became a sheet metal workshop, the owner was interested in spiritualism and it is said that he often held seances there.

During certain hours of the day it was impossible to do any work in one particular office, because of the inexplicable happenings which took place. A tin of paint was mysteriously flung across the office, denting a door and bursting open on the carpet. A heavy desk moved right across the room of its own accord, telephones were dashed against the walls and heavy cabinets toppled over.

A local vicar exorcized the place and although these occurrences are not as frequent, nor as drastic as on earlier occasions, strange things still happen from time to time, I'm told.

The showrooms of the Yorkshire Electricity Board in Mexborough have a record of odd happenings, which have taken place over the past twenty-five years or so, according to Mr C.R. Pocklington, who worked for the YEB in various capacities for twenty-seven years, until his retirement in 1974. He spent the last sixteen as a salesman in the Mexborough shop, and says:

'Over the years a lady assistant became such a bag of nerves, she had to retire early. A male assistant, who though normal enough when he commenced at the shop, soon required intensive psychiatric treatment and a young female assistant who was married at the age of twenty-one, became a widow less than three weeks later.'

Mr Pocklington himself had very little time off work through ill health, but in 1959 he suffered a stroke which robbed him of the use of one eye and put him off work for nine weeks. He continues: 'We eventually brought these happenings to the attention of the Area Manager, because we felt they were too much of a coincidence and because we felt there was something malevolent about the shop. The Area Manager was sceptical and said that these things could have happened anywhere.'

Some time in 1969, Mr Pocklington was alone in the shop, the other two assistants having gone to lunch, when a man came in and made a purchase from the 'small items' counter on the left of the shop floor. Mr Pocklington took the cash from the customer and, as he did so, saw a lady bending over a display in the centre of the shop floor. He told me: 'She was dressed entirely in a black, shiny material, with a broad hem on the jacket and three parts of the skirt. She wore black stockings and a good pair of black shoes. I couldn't see her face.'

Telling the lady he would only keep her waiting a second or two, Mr Pocklington turned around to put the cash from the man's purchase in the cash register behind him, a mere two or three seconds, and then turned back to serve the lady, but she had disappeared. She could not have got out of the shop in the length of time it took to put the money in the cash register and although Mr Pocklington searched the shop and looked outside, he says he could find no trace of her.

Was this the malevolent spirit which had caused so much distress in the past? Or was it the ghost of some previous occupant of the site? It appears, so far as I can ascertain, that the premises were built in 1936 on ground which was barren with no record of any previous building on the site. Mr Pocklington told me that as a boy he used to walk over the land occasionally on his way to the local grammar school during the period 1924-28. So we will probably never know the origin of the spectre, nor who or what caused the mysterious sounds of movement on the lower level of the showroom floor, or why the shop would some-times go very cold for no apparent reason. At the time of writing, the YEB have moved to new premises and this shop is now empty.

Not far from the centre of Huddersfield there used to be a cinema which rejoiced in the title of 'The Grand'. Over the years it has seen a number of changes, graduating from a dance hall and bingo hall, until today it is in use as a night club. Some time ago, Mrs Madeline Dannott and her husband were employed at the club and she related a number of rather unusual experiences they had while working there.

On more than one occasion they heard footsteps on the balcony, but on investigation found no one. Doors opened and closed by themselves and the sound of breaking glass was often heard, but again on investigation, nothing appeared to have been disturbed or damaged. Mrs Dannott told me: 'It was alleged in the local newspapers that only men heard these noises, but I know that I too have heard them.' What causes these ghostly noises?

It is thought to be the ghost of an elderly woman and goes back to the days when the club was a bingo hall. Apparently, in those days a person having a large win at bingo had to return at a later date to collect their winnings. The lady in question appears to have won quite a sizeable amount, but it seems that the excitement proved too much for her and she was called to her maker, before she had time to call for her winnings. So now she haunts the passage near the room where the money would have been paid out, supposedly seeking her night's winnings. A dedicated bingo fan indeed!

The Leeds Library, which was founded as far back as 1768, is the oldest organization of its kind in the country and it was in this old and dignified building that the ghost of a former librarian, Thomas Sternberg, was allegedly seen late in the last century.

Thomas Sternberg was appointed librarian in 1857 and died in office in 1879. He was a fine, handsome man with a good head of hair, close-cropped beard and moustache; erect, suave and very courteous. He was, in effect, a ladies' man who was well liked and respected by staff and public alike. Following his death, John MacAlister, sub-librarian of the Liverpool Library was appointed as his successor and it was he who was to have the first sighting of old Mr Sternberg's ghost.

Late one evening in the spring of 1884, MacAlister was alone in the library. He was working in his office, which was separated from the main library by a short passage. In those days the building was lit by gas and as the main room was in darkness, MacAlister had to use a lamp to find his way from his office, through the main room which, like his office, was on the first floor, down the stairs and through the ground floor room to the street when he was ready to leave. Noticing the late hour, he decided he must leave at once if he was to catch the last train home to Harrogate.

Picking up his lamp, he turned into the passage leading to the library proper and, to his surprise, he saw at the far end of it what appeared to be a man's face. His first thoughts were that a thief had broken into the building. He turned back to his room and took a revolver from his safe and then, holding the lamp behind him, he made his way along the passage and into the room. He saw no one at first, but as he moved cautiously past the rows of bookcases, he saw the face peering around the end of a row. It had an odd appearance, as if the body were inside the bookcase with just the head sticking out. The face was pallid and hairless and the orbits of the eyes were very deep. He advanced towards it and as he did so, he saw a man with high shoulders who seemed to rotate out of the end of the bookcase and, with his back towards him, walk with a rather quick shuffling gait, from the bookcase to the door of a small lavatory.

He heard no noise and following the man quickly into the lavatory was surprised to find no one there. MacAlister confessed later to experiencing then, for the first time, an eerie feeling. Quickly he left the library, only to discover he had missed his last train.

The following morning he mentioned what he had seen,

to the Rev Charles Hargrove, a member of the Library
Committee, who after listening politely suggested that the
description fitted that of Thomas Sternberg. The ghost was
seen several times after that by various members of staff,
but to my knowledge it has not been seen this century. Why
it should suddenly appear and just as suddenly cease to
haunt the library is beyond me. Perhaps it is sufficient to
relate that the ghost was never seen again after 1887, when
John MacAlister left to take up another appointment in
London.

Another library which provides us with a more up-to-date
ghost story, is that at the York Museum, where at 7.40 one
Sunday evening in September 1953, a strange thing
happened which was to result in a great deal of publicity in
the national press.

On the evening in question George Jonas, the caretaker,
was waiting for a meeting to finish and was sitting enjoying
a quiet cup of tea. Eventually the meeting ended and after
seeing everyone off the premises, Mr Jonas set out to make
a final check on the building before leaving himself. As he
left his room, he heard footsteps and thinking the curator
was still in his office, went to speak to him. However, instead
of finding the curator, Mr Jonas was confronted by a complete stranger, busily engaged in searching for something in
the museum office.

The man was bent over in the far corner of the room. He
straightened up as the caretaker walked in, turned round
and walked out of the room, passing Mr Jonas as he did so.
Mr Jonas at first thought that it was someone who had
stayed behind after the meeting. He followed the man out
of the room, remaining a few steps behind him. He later
told the press, 'I noticed then that he was dressed in a frock
coat and drainpipe trousers, rather like an old professor;
and wore elastic-sided boots. I noticed this quite distinctly,

as there were no turn-ups on his trousers.' Mr Jonas then went on to describe how he had followed the figure into the library, turning on the lights as he did so, and heard the man speaking slowly, as if to himself, saying, 'I must find it —I must find it!'

The figure moved about from bookshelf to bookshelf, rummaging among the volumes and Mr Jonas went up to him and said, 'If you want to see the curator, I'll escort you across to his house.' As he spoke, he reached out to touch the man's arm, but as he did so the figure simply vanished, much to his bewilderment. Before vanishing, the man dropped a volume he had withdrawn from the shelf, the title of which was *Antiques and Curiosities of the Church*. The caretaker left the book where it had fallen and the following morning told the whole incredible story to the curator.

Four Sundays later Mr Jonas saw the apparition again. The figure of the old man crossed the hall and simply faded through the locked doors and into the library. Again, a month later Mr Jonas and a friend heard the turning of pages and saw the identical book drop to the floor. It now became obvious that proper investigations should be carried out to determine just who the phantom reader was and, as a result, six people gathered in the museum's library one Sunday evening in December 1953, and sat waiting for the ghostly apparition. A careful check had been made beforehand and all present, a doctor, a solicitor, Mr Jonas and his brother and two representatives of the press, agreed that any form of trickery was out of the question.

On previous occasions the ghost had appeared at exactly 7.40 P.M. but on this occasion it was 7.48 when the first phenomena occurred and the gathering heard a rubbing sound and saw a book slowly withdraw from the shelf and drop to the floor, remaining in an upright position. No figure was seen, but the watchers felt their legs become uncomfortably cold up to the knees and all present were convinced that they had been witness to the activity of a supernatural agency.

Whose ghost was this? Theory had it that it was the apparition of Alderman Edward Wooler, a Darlington solicitor and antiquary who had died in 1921 and who had owned the book in question. However, since that night in December 1953, the ghost has never been seen, so it has not been possible for positive identification to be made. Several people have investigated in recent years, but have reported nothing other than the feeling of unnatural coldness.

While I was on a visit to Hull in 1972, a relative, knowing of my interest in ghosts and the supernatural, took me to a smart hair-dressing salon in Whitefriargate, not far from Paragon station in the city centre. I don't know whether the salon is still there, but at that time the ghostly activities of an anonymous and noisy phantom were causing something of a stir in the town.

If I remember correctly, the owners were then a Mr and Mrs Hardy or Hartley. They had become so disturbed late in 1971 by mysterious noises coming from an upstairs room that they had called the police. The sounds, which had been heard by customers and staff alike, were those of someone slowly pacing the floor of the empty room and dragging something towards the door. This was followed by further shufflings and scuffling.

The police had to admit that they were baffled by it all, but they locked the door and fitted trip wires. They were even more baffled when the sounds continued and when, on opening up the room, they found it remained undisturbed, although the lights had been mysteriously switched on. Investigations by the police, the local press and others, including the author, have failed to come up with any

reasonable explanation for the unaccount
continued for some time after that and, for
still being heard.

The *Wharfedale and Airedale Observer* of 1883 tell a
mysterious happening which took place in a small cobbler's
workshop in the village of Timble, on the southern slopes
of the Washburn valley, in 1825.

In that year, a young shoemaker called William Holmes
rented a small house and workshop, where he lived and
worked alone. Like most cobblers and shoemakers of that
time, he used a glue which was kept in a sizing tin. In the
course of time, he noticed that on some mornings the sizing
tin, which he had left empty the previous night, was filled
with leather parings and odd scraps from his workbench.
Soon it began to be filled regularly and he noticed that on
top of the tin there were always two long strips laid cross-
wise.

At first William Holmes thought it was the local village
lads playing tricks on him, so he began to lock and shutter
his windows at night as well as his door, and he made sure
before he went to bed each night that the glue tin was
empty. However, the next morning the tin would again be
filled.

One night he balanced the tin on an upright iron rod
which he had driven into a wooden block. The slightest
touch would upset it. Needless to say, the following
morning the tin was found to be filled, but remained undisturbed, precariously balanced, as he had left it the
previous night.

Next, Holmes decided that each night he would sweep up
every scrap of leather left over from his day's work. It made
not the slightest difference, except that now the tin was
found to be full of an assortment of broken glass and bits of
wood and it still had the usual cross on top. William Holmes

was, to say the least, perplexed. He went to discuss his problem with the local vicar, who agreed that with his friend the village tailor, he would stay the night at the house and try to solve the mystery.

So, a few nights later, the vicar and the tailor stayed in the house, sitting up all night while William got some sleep. The next morning, both the vicar and the tailor testified to hearing a noise during the night which sounded like quick, short breathing. They also shamefully confessed to being too afraid to go down to the workshop to investigate. Holmes said he slept soundly all night and heard nothing. The tin in the meantime had been filled up again.

Some weeks later, Holmes having finished his evening meal decided to go and visit one of his near neighbours. He went out of the house, locking the door behind him. On returning later that night, he was surprised to find the tin was partly filled, and for the first time he began to feel frightened. He gave up renting the house and moved to lodgings elsewhere and the mystery of the tidying-up ghost, or whatever it was, was never solved, although William Holmes, in later years a successful farmer, told the story up until the day he died in 1850. He always maintained that the ghost was that of Tommy Kaye, an idiot boy who had lived in the village, but had died several years before these events took place. Even as late as 1883 there were still a number of people living in the village who remembered the curious incident.

RAF Lindholme at Hatfield, near Doncaster, was haunted by the ghost of a big man in aircrew uniform. It first made its appearance in 1947 when a group of airmen returning to the base saw it walking out on the marshes nearby. It soon became known as 'Lindholme Willie' by both airmen and local people, several of whom have seen it in more recent years.

The villagers of Hatfield believe the ghost to be that of an airman killed in a crash on the marshes during the Second World War and every description of him has been the same. In November 1957, a corporal in Air Traffic Control at the base reported seeing 'Willie's' misty shape walking on the runway, having come from the direction of the marshes. Knowing an aircraft was due to land and thinking someone had strayed on to the runway, he radioed control to alert them, but before he could take a closer look, the figure vanished.

Another ghost, which sets off a burglar alarm for no apparent reason, is giving the staff at one Town Hall in North Yorkshire the creeps. Members of the Town Hall staff say it could be the pranks of a ghost called 'Oscar'. Even security experts cannot guess what makes the flashing light alarm at the Town Hall go haywire from time to time. The Mayor has said that the warning lights go on in the Town Hall, but not in the local police station as they should. Some people who have investigated have reported seeing a strange figure lurking in the shadows.

Who was 'Oscar'? My own enquiries lead me to believe he was a man who was arrested for fighting in a drunken brawl sometime during the 1880s and who hanged himself in the police cells, which used to be below the Town Hall, now probably trying to get his own back.

On a June night in 1956, seven workmen settled down to sleep in makeshift beds and sleeping bags which had been provided for them on the ground floor of Watton Abbey, near Driffield. The owner was selling up after a tenancy of over thirty years and the workmen had come up from Retford in Nottinghamshire to help with the three-day sale of furniture and fittings of the old abbey.

A fierce June wind howled around the reputedly haunted

building as they slept. Then, at about one o'clock in the
morning, above the high wind could be heard the eerie
tolling of a bell. Every one of the workmen awoke at once
and sat bolt upright in their beds, spines tingling and the
hair rising at the back of their necks, for they knew that the
abbey bell had been removed many years before.

One man was so afraid that he dived head first through a
window, injuring himself when he landed in a flower bed.
The auctioneer's foreman in charge of the men grabbed a
shot-gun, loaded it and fired off both barrels skywards.
This had the desired effect and the bell suddenly ceased its
tolling. As one, the men picked up their beds and bedrolls
and spent the remainder of the night in a large marquee
which had been erected in the grounds of the abbey to hold
the auction. They were taking no chances, for there was no
doubt in their minds that the ringing was the work of the
headless ghost of Watton, the nun, Elfrida (see Chapter 7).

As I began this chapter with a haunted broadcasting studio,
so I will end it.

'The staff at BBC Radio Leeds have for years worked
alongside a ghost and flying kettle lids and eerie footsteps
are accepted nowadays without question.' So says Caroline
Woodruff, now of BBC Radio Manchester.

The BBC took over Broadcasting House in Woodhill
Lane some time in the 1930s, and even at this time
members of staff were claiming to have seen the hooded
figure of the so-called 'Grey Lady' gliding across the gallery
into studio two and disappearing through the opposite
wall. The 'Grey Lady' apparently gets her name from the
fact that she has never been seen in colour, but in varying
shades of grey and black. She moves just above the ground,
something which is accounted for by the fact that the
ground levels of the building were altered when the 'Beeb'
took over. Today, no one claims to have witnessed the

ghost, but other unaccountable sights and sensations have led a number of employees to refuse to work alone in this part of the building.

Seventy-six-year-old Albert Aldred recalled working at the studios during the Second World War and hearing footsteps in the gallery at night when no one else was in the place. He said they sounded more as if they were walking on carpet, rather than on the present stone floor. He knew a lot of the staff in those days used to hear things and some of them actually resigned through fear.

In December 1978, Sharon Carter began work at the studios as a part-time receptionist. Now she refuses to enter the upstairs restroom. She said, 'I wouldn't go into that room again after what happened to me.' Apparently, one Sunday evening just before seven o'clock, Sharon was in the restroom talking to a friend on the telephone. There was a kettle on the floor and for no reason at all the lid suddenly turned round and flew across the room, landing in the sink at the other side with a resounding crash. Sharon said, 'There was no one else around and I certainly didn't put it there. The room had been very cold where I had been sitting, but it was really warm in the area around the sink.'

Caroline Woodruff told me that when she was working at Radio Leeds, a member of the Radio Leeds newsroom staff arrived for work early one morning to find tapes and papers strewn across the room for no apparent reason; and a typewriter had been overturned. Many of the staff find the building a little eerie at night and Caroline, then a station assistant, was working there one Sunday night, when she got a distinctly cold feeling around her. She told me: 'I was not imagining things. Although it was eleven o'clock at night and I was the only person in the place, I got the feeling that I was not alone. I jolly soon picked up the tapes I was editing and took them down into the studios to finish them.'

Caroline said that after that, she would not edit at the studios at night, nor would she go into studio two, next to the gallery at night either.

Investigations have consistently failed to shed any light on the ghost or its origins. There is, however, a theory that the 'Grey Lady' is in some way connected with the Quakers who occupied the building before the BBC took it over. She does seem to appear most often on a Sunday, so perhaps she feels that the staff would be better engaged in religious activities rather than working on the Sabbath. However, the present staff do not view her as a threat in any way.

What one might call a 'radio active' ghost, perhaps?

CHAPTER 2

Mysterious Grey Ladies

The visitor to Yorkshire is well catered for when it comes to stately homes, castles, country houses and halls. Nearly all of which have their resident grey lady. In many cases the reason behind the haunting has been lost in the mists of time, or the details have become distorted over the years in the re-telling. Even the identity of the ghost in question is often shrouded in mystery or in a mixture of fact and fantasy. Many of the ghosts in this chapter have never been seen by anyone within living memory, but others, the ghosts of older private houses and farms, have been seen recently and will continue to be seen for some time to come.

Rose Cottage stands in a small village near Halifax and was for some years the home of the daughter of Mr C. Robinson of Norton Tower, Halifax, to whom I am indebted for the following story.

It appears that the cottage was built on the site of an old Quaker chapel and when, in the course of time, parts of the cottage were knocked down and a kitchen extension and bathroom were built, this encroached on the old graveyard and may have been the cause of the frequent manifestations which the family afterwards witnessed.

Mr Robinson told me: 'When my daughter was expecting and towards the end of her pregnancy, she was unable to sleep too well at night. So as not to keep disturbing her husband, she decided to sleep downstairs on the large settee. One night she woke up and was surprised to see a lady, dressed in a long dark dress with white collar and cuffs, standing at one end of the settee, looking down at her.' She was not in the least frightened by this and even forgot about it, neglecting to tell her husband. Some time later the cottage was sold to a couple who had lived for many years in Australia, and who had returned to this country on retirement.

Mr Robinson continued: 'A few weeks after moving in, my son-in-law happened to meet the new owners and they asked him why he hadn't mentioned the ghost to them. Tony, my son-in-law, had not experienced it and admitted he knew nothing about it.' Apparently, the ghost of the woman had been seen quite frequently by the new owners. She would just appear and stand looking at them for about a minute, before fading away. Their fourteen-year-old niece had also seen it and a nephew almost walked into the ghost in the passage.

'One weekend,' said Mr Robinson, 'the wife took ill. Her husband spent the first night of her illness in the small bedroom and awoke in the early hours to find the ghost of the woman standing at the foot of his bed. Her arms were folded and she appeared to be shaking her head as if to say, "I am very sorry." The man was most alarmed at this, for he took it to mean that something was going to happen to his wife.'

It didn't. The ghost was in fact referring to him, for exactly two weeks later the poor man collapsed and died!

A far happier spectre was seen by eleven-year-old Philip Lawton one winter's evening in 1945 when, with his parents, he lived on a farm above Huddersfield. Parts of the building dated back to the sixteenth century. Mr Lawton told me: 'I lived in one of the farm cottages, across the yard from the old farmhouse itself, which was occupied by my uncle. On this particular evening I was asked to take something across to the house for my uncle. In crossing the yard, I had to pass an old coach house, the huge doors of which had long since disappeared.'

Passing the entrance to this old building, he happened to glance in and a movement from inside caught his eye, causing him to stop and look closer. Coming out of the doorway was a stout woman, wearing a long blue dress over the front of which was a white apron. On her head she wore what he could only describe as a 'mob cap' and she was carrying a large basket containing what appeared to be laundry. Mr Lawton continued: 'I can see her now in my mind, so clearly. She came to within a yard of where I was standing and then she just smiled at me and vanished. I can clearly remember the scent of cleanliness, a soapy odour which surrounded her. Her arms were fat and red, as was her face.'

He said he was not the least bit afraid. The whole thing lasted for no more than half a minute, but it was, to his young mind, a pleasant and in a sense a comforting experience. The identity of the ghostly lady remains a mystery, but does it really matter who she is? To house such a friendly shade of the past just adds to the attraction of these old Yorkshire farming communities.

Standing on the right-hand side of Thornhill Road in Rastrick are two delightful cottages, which are thought to have been converted from an inn, built in 1690 on the site of earlier premises. My family and I spent a pleasant afternoon here in the spring of 1980, discussing with Mr and Mrs Auty, the present occupiers, some of the strange goings-on which had occurred over the past six years.

Marilyn Auty told me that the occurrences began shortly after they had moved into the house in November 1974. At first she used to hear a low whistling noise which continued on and off for several weeks, until it became loud enough to be heard over the noise of the television and was accompanied by an annoying tapping sound, which seemed to emanate from the lounge ceiling and move from one end of the room to the other. It continued for periods lasting several hours.

More recently a figure had been seen and a mysterious fine film of swirling smoke. Mrs Auty said, 'My husband had just retired to bed one night recently and I was tidying up downstairs before going up myself. As I went to turn out the lounge light, I saw what appeared to be a fine film of smoke near the front door, which swirled for a few seconds before disappearing.' Some days later she was vacuuming upstairs, when from the lounge came a loud tapping noise as if someone was knocking with a coin on a pane of glass. Thinking someone was at the front door, Mrs Auty went downstairs only to find no one at either the front or back door. Puzzled, she began to go back upstairs and on nearing the landing saw a 'long, thin, filmy, cloudlike thing' glide straight past her and cross the top of the stairs from one landing to the other. By the time she reached the top it had vanished.

That evening, over dinner Marilyn Auty started to tell her husband of her experience. For a while he listened politely and then suddenly his face changed. She said, 'He looked straight past me and fixed his gaze on something behind me.' This was at a very large and very old picture on the wall which was visibly swaying from side to side.

Her husband told me that he always felt as though someone was watching. There was often a strange atmosphere on the stairs and Mrs Auty's sister refused to go up them whenever she visited the house. People had told them that while they were away from the house, a figure was seen peering through the bedroom window at the front. Was this the same figure that had been seen by Mr Auty? He told me, 'Marilyn was in hospital at the time. I had been to visit her and arriving home at about 8 o'clock, I made myself a snack and sat on the settee to eat it. Suddenly, from the door leading to the kitchen a woman in grey floated across the room and vanished near the front door. She wore a cloak over her grey dress and appeared to have been cut off at the knees.' The floor in this room had been raised by Mr Auty, who is a joiner, with the original flagged floor remaining intact beneath it. During our visit I made several attempts to photograph Mr and Mrs Auty near the doorway where the figure entered. On each occasion my flash gun failed to operate and it was only after I had asked them to sit in a different place that I was able to obtain my photograph.

About a week after our visit, Marilyn Auty wrote to me to tell me of an incident which happened just after we had left. She said, 'After your visit, my husband went to do some work in his garden whilst I remained in the lounge. About an hour had elapsed, when I heard someone call my name. As I got up from the chair I heard it again, very clearly and sounding most perturbed. Thinking it was my husband, I rushed into the kitchen only to find it empty and I could see him busy digging at the bottom of the garden.'

Who or what haunts this cottage is obviously friendly towards the young couple and although these occurrences startle them from time to time, they are in no way afraid. Why should they be, the house has a lovely friendly atmosphere about it.

Not so with Greenfield Lodge though. Greenfield Lodge, well known amongst hikers and cyclists for its cuisine, stands high above the reservoirs on Rishworth Moor near Scammonden dam. It is a fifteen-roomed Georgian house with Victorian additions and when originally built was called 'Red House'. In 1847, it became known as Greenfield Lodge and then, around 1860 when a barn and stables were added, it was renamed 'Parkfield Hall', although for some reason it has reverted to the name of Greenfield Lodge.

During the past twenty-odd years, while it has been occupied by its present owners, a number of strange incidents have occurred. Until recent years when they began to keep cows for their own milk production, milk was delivered from a farm nearby. One morning, the lady who delivered it was making her way to the Lodge in her Land-rover and had the feeling she was not alone in the vehicle. When she pulled up outside Greenfield Lodge, she was terrified to see the passenger door open and close by itself, as if an invisible passenger had got out. On another occasion, the screech of brakes on the road outside late at night, caused the occupants of the Lodge to dash to the bedroom windows to see what had happened. I was told that a car had come to a grinding halt in the middle of the road and the driver, a man, was examining the orchard gate, directly opposite the house. The gates were securely fastened, but his passenger, a young woman, appeared to be very frightened for she was heard to say, 'Come on, let's get out of here,' and, pointing to Greenfield Lodge, 'It came from out of there.' The man got into the car which sped off noisily into the night.

Could this have been a reoccurrence of something which happened twenty years earlier? When the family were moving in, the husband had brought a trailer load of furniture from their home in Rotherham and as it was rather late he decided to bed down for the night at Green-field Lodge.

He was awakened during the small hours by the sound of children. It seemed quite light outside and on looking out of the window he saw a group of children singing and shouting in the forecourt and completely ignoring the car and trailer parked there. He watched as the group then walked down towards the Brown Cow Inn a few hundred yards away, across the road to the gates of Mount Pleasant Farm and then back towards the stables of Greenfield Lodge, before vanishing as if into thin air. No one knows to this day who those children were, but later investigations show that many years ago the Lodge had been inhabited by an order of monks, who used it as a children's home and the ten stables, now in ruins, had been in use as dormitories.

The house itself has a more interesting spectre, thought to be the ghost of Elizabeth Emmet who, in 1834 (as far as I can make out from the mass of legal documents I was allowed to examine during my visit to the house), either came into possession of Greenfield Lodge or died there during that year. The ghost invariably appears whenever some work is about to be undertaken, or when alterations are made to the house. She wears a long grey skirt and a high-necked blouse with a row of buttons down the front. Her hair is parted down the centre and fastened in a bun on the top of her head. However, it is not possible to make out her features, for invariably her hands appear to be covering her face as if she is weeping uncontrollably.

On another occasion, the family were away and a friend of theirs was staying to look after the house. She was sitting alone on the settee in the dining room, when the kitchen door at one end of the room opened and closed. She sensed someone or something cross the room, which had turned extremely cold, and then, to her utter amazement, the door which leads into the hall also opened and closed.

For many years, the house has had one room which is used as a café. One afternoon, a coachload of women arrived for afternoon tea. As they were about to leave, a woman was seen to come out of the living room, where no one should have been, and go upstairs. The bus driver called to see if all were on the coach and he was told to wait because someone had been seen going upstairs. Investigation proved that no one was there, although there was no

way in which she could have got out again without being
seen.

Many times visitors to the house have heard noises upstairs, as if a person is moving about. These noises occur at
all times of the day and night. A woman's voice can often be
heard, although muffled, repeating a single word. In one
corner of the living room, the lovely aroma of fish and chips
can often be smelled, as if wafting up from the cellar
underneath where some old fire ovens have been discovered recently. The sound of a car stopping outside,
when the road is empty and other mysterious happenings
which one is hard put to explain, make this one of the most
interesting houses I have visited during my researches.
And although the family are exceptionally warm and
friendly people who made me more than welcome, I got
the feeling that the house itself is not friendly towards
prying strangers. Even though it was a nice warm day, the
house felt chilled and I regret to say that I was not sorry to
turn my back on it.

Mrs Constance Drake of Halifax related an interesting
story concerning a close friend of hers whose husband was
the resident caretaker of Kirkby Hall, near York.

The Hall, the seat of the Crowther family, was built
about 1750 alongside a Tudor dwelling which became an
integral part, although most of the Tudor fabric was pulled
down around 1949–50. Parts of the house surrounded an
old cobbled courtyard and all the bedrooms that were in
use overlooked the courtyard and outbuildings. In what is
now called the dairy there is often a lovely smell of fresh
baked bread, suggesting perhaps that this might have been
a kitchen or bakehouse in days gone by. In the stone-
flagged passageways on the ground floor the sound of
running children's feet and the delicious rustle of silk, as if

someone is chasing them, has been heard on several occasions.

Once, Mrs Clark, the caretaker's wife, expecting members of the Crowther family to return from a holiday, went into the library with the intention of giving it a good clean and polish and was more than horrified at the sight which met her eyes. The room looked as if a hurricane had blown through it. Papers were scattered, books had fallen from the shelves, ornaments appeared to have been thrown about, and on a small table lay a battered book, opened at a poem which she paused to read. Later, having tidied up, Mrs Clark fastened the room up and went about her other duties. Later in the day, she had occasion to go to the library for something and was dismayed to find that again it was in a state of disarray and the book was again lying open on the table, at the same page. No one has ever been able to explain the significance of this.

By far the most interesting experience happened several months later. Mrs Crowther had received a letter from an elderly lady who lived away from the area and who had been associated with the house in her younger days. The lady said that she would like a last look at the house before she died, as it had such happy memories. As Mrs Crowther knew the lady she replied that she was most welcome to look over the house again, but that she herself would not be at home and the caretaker's wife would receive her.

Mrs Clark was instructed that the elderly lady would be driving herself up to the house on a certain day and she was to be made to feel at home, be shown round the house and be given a cup of tea. The day duly arrived and as it wore on, it seemed that the visitor was not going to call after all. By 11.30 that night, Mrs Clark knew there was no chance of her coming that day and retired to bed.

At about 2 in the morning Mrs Clark was awoken by the

sound of a car and saw the reflection of headlights in the room. Getting out of bed and looking through the window, she was surprised to see a Standard Vanguard draw up in the courtyard and a white-haired lady get out and close the car door with a bang. Mrs Clark opened the window to call out that she would come down to the front door, when the woman suddenly got back into the car and drove off. It was only afterwards that Mrs Clark realized the car had driven straight through the locked gates!

The following morning Mrs Crowther telephoned and Mrs Clark told her what had happened, that the visitor had come late in the night and had driven off before she could open the door. Mrs Clark was quite taken aback when she was informed by Mrs Crowther that it was not possible, for the old lady had been killed at 2 o'clock the previous afternoon, when her Standard Vanguard had been in a collision with another vehicle.

In 1934, a nineteen-year-old girl, whom to respect her wish to remain anonymous I will call Gemma, went to work at Nafferton Hall, between Driffield and Bridlington, as a domestic maid. She told me: 'It was in the middle of winter. I knew very little of Nafferton, coming as I did from some miles away and I knew very little about the Hall.'

As was customary for maids of that period, Gemma was given a bedroom in the attic. The Hall had been converted to electricity by this time, but the cellars and the servants' quarters had not been connected up and therefore they still had to use candles. Gemma continued: 'On going to bed on my very first night there, I had an odd sort of feeling. I can't say I felt frightened, more uncomfortable really. I did not like the room I had been given and after a few nights I took the precaution of wedging a pen-knife in the latch, so that it could not be opened. We had no locks on the doors. One night I felt so uncomfortable, I lit my candle with my eyes shut as I was afraid of what I might see in the dark.'

She says she had the same feeling in the cellars, in particular the apple cellar. She hated going in there. There was a large slab in the cellar floor with a ring in it, which was said to be the entrance to an underground passage. The door to the apple cellar was always open and this frightened the young girl, who had to pass it every time she went to the dairy. However, more of this later. After a while, Gemma made friends with the cook and mentioned to her the feelings she had both in her room and in the cellar. The cook told her that she had heard tales of a 'white lady' haunting the Hall. Gemma says 'I never saw her, but I got the feeling she was connected with my bedroom in some way and that she was watching me whenever I was in there.'

The following summer, two young men came to spend the weekend at Nafferton Hall. They were students and friends of the family, who used to be invited quite often. On this particular occasion, they were to sleep in the empty room immediately beneath the attic room where Gemma slept. She said, 'During the night, I suddenly heard them jump out of bed and go racing downstairs. I heard a window open and the chain and bolt on the front door rattle. All was quiet for a short time and then the window was closed and I heard the students come back to their room.'

Serving breakfast the following morning she overheard a member of the household saying she had heard the two students opening the door during the night. To which the students replied that they had not, they had gone through the window as it was quicker, and followed the figure of a white lady across the lawn, where she suddenly disappeared. Gemma heard no more of this particular conversation as she had to return, rather reluctantly, to the kitchen. She said, 'I gathered they had slept in that particular room with the intention of sighting the ghost of Nafferton Hall.'

Time passed and Gemma could not shake off the feeling of being watched. By October of that year she had become very nervous and decided that she must give in her notice. While she was working out her notice, she was in the house alone one afternoon, having been given strict instructions to have the tea ready at a certain time for when the family returned. She began to prepare the tea when she discovered that there was no butter or milk and she would have to go down into the dairy, in the cellars. Taking up a candle, she set off into the cellars and as she passed the apple cellar door, which was again open, she paused to close and fasten it. 'It fastened with a chain and padlock,' she said, 'although I did not padlock it as that would have meant trouble from the family. I just put the chain over the staple and hooked the padlock through.'

Feeling much better with that door shut, Gemma went on her way to the dairy. On her way back, however, she nearly fainted when she saw that the door was once again open. She hadn't heard the chain fall, which she says she would surely have done if it had come open by itself.

Gemma dashed terrified to the kitchen, leaving her candle to burn itself out in the dairy as she dared not go back for it. Needless to say, she was in trouble when the family returned for not having got the tea ready, but she did not tell them why. She tells me that this is something that she has regretted ever since, for had she asked, she might have learnt the story behind the ghost of Nafferton Hall, although she says, 'Perhaps I was too afraid to want to know at that time.'

Another strange incident occurred just before she left which has mystified her ever since. One night she heard a noise which she tells me sounded rather like a cockerel, but with a funny crow. She says that she heard the noise two or three times, but could never make up her mind as to just what it was. One thing Gemma is sure about though, she was very relieved to leave Nafferton Hall. She said finally, 'I did not see a ghost, but there was something very uncanny there. I had never been afraid of attic bedrooms before or since, whether they were lit by candle or electricity. As a matter of fact, I would sit in the dark by the open window and listen to the owls hooting, so I couldn't understand why I shouldn't like Nafferton Hall.'

So much for the personal stories, but what about the other, better known grey ladies who haunt Yorkshire and whom we all know about, but very few of us can claim to have seen? For instance, the ghost which haunts the fifteenth-century home of the Metcalfe family, Nappa Hall at Askrigg, which has been recorded as being seen wearing a Tudor-style dress and cap and is generally thought to be the pathetic and heartbroken spectre of that lovely, but unhappy royal prisoner Mary Queen of Scots. She is said to have spent a couple of nights here, sleeping in the massive oak bed, which has been preserved. Although she is known to have been kept a prisoner at Bolton Castle for about six months in 1568, there is some doubt as to whether she did actually stay at Nappa Hall, or indeed whether this ghost is really hers. Like her cousin, Elizabeth I and Anne Boleyn, Mary's alleged ghost is one of the most popular phantoms in the country.

East Riddlesden Hall, a seventeenth-century manor house situated within a few yards of the busy A560 at Keighley, is haunted by an unidentified female, wearing a long blue dress which can be heard swishing about as she walks aimlessly along corridors and in and out of rooms. This old Hall was originally owned by the Rishworth family, and in one of the rooms can still be seen a carved wooden cradle, used for rocking their children. I was told recently that this cradle has been seen rocking, without being touched by human hands. Perhaps these were the hands of the mysterious lady in blue.

Mrs A. Townsend of Keighley related an interesting experience she and her daughter had while visiting the Hall about ten years ago. She told me: 'After looking round the house and the grounds, we went into the old barn where an old stage coach was kept. As I made to go towards it to have a look inside, I suddenly went very cold and felt as if something was holding me back and I was not able to go any further. My daughter shouted for me to come out as she didn't like it in there and felt very much afraid.'

Another correspondent, Mr M. Atkins of Whitby, had an even more unusual experience at the Hall in December 1963. At the time, Mr Atkins was a taxi driver and one night he was called out to pick up a fare from the Hall. He said, 'There is a large stone porch and when I got there it was quite dark with no lights either in the porch or the grounds. I couldn't find the bell-push in the dark, so I went and peered through one of the windows nearby.'

He was surprised to see, inside the room, a lady in period dress, but as it was near Christmas he assumed there must be a fancy dress party going on. Going back to the door, he found it was not locked so he let himself in to the large reception hall. There was no one about and he thought how strange it was for a party to be going on, yet the place was as quiet as a church, except for some music coming faintly from somewhere down a long passage. Following the sound he found himself in the caretaker's room where he found a lady waiting for him to take her home in his taxi. He continued, 'In the taxi I said to the lady I thought there was a party going on and told her what I had seen through the window. She sat quiet for a time and then said, "Do you know, you have seen a ghost." ' Mr Atkins said to me later that he is not a very good story-teller, nor is he a great believer in ghosts, but as he said, 'One thing I do know, that woman was there in the Hall all right.'

Had Mr Atkins seen the lady in blue? If so who was she? Was she a member of the Rishworth family or was she a nanny, who like many an unfortunate young woman before and since met a tragic end?

Another lady in blue, this time elderly, haunts Temple Newsham House, near Leeds. Lord Halifax, who lived there until 1922, is said to have observed her, when on a winter's night in 1908, the firelight in his bedroom revealed a woman with a shawl draped over her shoulders, crossing the room and vanishing into an adjoining one. Screams of agony have also been heard in this part of the house. The house, which is said to have been the birthplace of Henry, Lord Darnley, husband of Mary Queen of Scots, has many other ghosts to its credit including a small boy who has been seen stepping out of a cupboard in the room where Darnley is thought to have been born.

An old house in Kirkgate, Wakefield, was said to have been haunted by a woman who had been locked up in one of the cramped little attic rooms, high under the chimneys and who starved to death when whoever locked her in forgot about her, either by accident or design.

While in the Wakefield area, mention should also be made of the ghost of old Lady Bolles of Old Heath Hall, who when she died in 1661, at the age of 83, left a very detailed will. £700 was left to be spent on mourning and £400 to cover funeral expenses. It must have been some funeral! Old Lady Bolles also left strict instructions that the door to the room in which she died was to be permanently sealed.

The room remained locked for a good number of years, but eventually a new occupant of the Hall, possibly not knowing of the old woman's wishes, opened it up again and in doing so disturbed the vengeance-seeking spirit of old Lady Bolles. Angry at her orders being disobeyed, her ghost haunted the Hall for the next two hundred years or more, until its demolition. Her most favoured haunt was the banqueting hall at Christmastime, where she was seen several times by a number of soldiers billeted there during the Second World War.

Now, all that is left of her old hall is the door to Lady Mary's bedroom, which is on display at Wakefield Museum. And her ghost? That was said to have been laid by a local vicar at a place called Bolles Pit, on the River Aire.

Castlegate House, close to York Minster, has a grey lady who has been seen climbing the stairs. Two other ghosts, thought to be former occupants, haunted Thornton Watlass. One was said to be dressed in eighteenth-century clothes and the other, a Victorian woman dressed in grey. Countersett Hall, near Hawse, is haunted by an unknown ghostly female, and an unknown ghost seen at North Kilvington, on the A19 north of Thirsk, was clad in white. Local gossip said she was the wraith of the seventeen-year-old daughter of Roger Meynell of Kilvington Hall, who was killed by soldiers in the Chapel of the Hall at the time of the Dissolution, and whose body was thrown into a stream.

Heights Farm at Rishworth is haunted by a ghost known as 'The Lady of the Heights'. A figure dressed in late Victorian clothes and thought to be the ghost of a lady who died there some years ago, has been seen quite frequently in the area.

Snape Castle, near Bedale, boasts a regal ghost, thought to be Catherine Parr, the last wife of Henry VIII. Over the past century, several people have claimed to have seen the ghost of a young girl dressed in Tudor-style dress, with long fair hair showing beneath a small white lace cap. She is said to appear happy and contented.

Spofforth is a charming little village between Wetherby and Harrogate, on the A661, and its castle was for centuries the home of the notorious Percy family, until things became a little too hot for them in these parts and they moved to Northumberland. William the Conqueror held William de Percy in high esteem and he provided him with a number of manors in Yorkshire, as payment for services rendered during the Conquest. Over the years the family's influence spread throughout Yorkshire and the North of England.

The castle, more a fortified manor than a traditional castle, has been a ruin since it was damaged by the Yorkists during the Wars of the Roses after its owner, the Earl of Northumberland, died in Towton. It then fell into decline during the early Tudor period and parts of it were dismantled. It was little more than its present ruin by the time of Elizabeth I. The tower, which still stands, is haunted by a spectre which has been seen quite often over the years and, indeed, was seen quite recently. The spectre appears at the top of the tower and after standing quite motionless for several minutes, it appears to throw itself off and plunges to the ground where it disappears. Only the top half of the figure is ever seen, and those who have seen it claim it is female.

According to Mr William Foggitt of Thirsk, a restless lady haunts Thirsk Hall, the home of Captain Peter Bell and his wife Hilary. This apparition has been seen several times by visitors, sleeping in the huge four-poster bed in the bedroom over-looking the parish church. The ghost is thought to be that of a young woman who through commiting suicide was refused burial in consecrated ground and was most probably buried beneath the Georgian hall.

Similarly, a poor victim of an insane and jealous husband roams about the ruins of Skipsea Castle, which stands near the junction of the B1242 and the B1249 between Bridlington and Hornsea. This is the ghost of Lady de Bevere, niece of William the Conqueror, who roams the castle in the vain hope of leading some hardy soul to her last resting place. It has been said that once someone follows her and retrieves her bones to give them a decent Christian burial, her tormented soul will find eternal rest.

Bolling Hall, a lovely old manor house near Bradford, boasts an anonymous ghost of a grey lady who was responsible for saving the lives of the whole population of the town during the Civil War.

In 1643, the Hall was owned by Richard Tempest, an ardent supporter of Charles I. It was beneath his roof that the Earl of Newcastle stayed the night after issuing grim orders for the massacre of every man, woman and child in Bradford. The town was a hotbed of Puritanism and lay under siege by the King's forces. The Earl of Newport had been killed during the laying of the siege and Newcastle was so incensed by this, he issued the now infamous order that, on the following day, his soldiers should 'put to the sword every man, woman and child, without regard to age or distinction whatsoever'.

That night the Earl slept badly, for he reported that three times the clothes were pulled from his bed and a ghostly female form appeared, dressed all in white, which appealed to him in 'piteous and lamentable tones' to 'pity poor Bradford'. Sceptics said the Earl was drunk. Others were not quite so polite and suggested that the female was not a ghost but a venturesome wench who lived nearby. Who or whatever it was, however, succeeded in persuading the

Earl to cancel the previous day's order and thus spare the poor citizens of Bradford.

One man who resided in Bradford during the siege was Joseph Lister, who was to write later, 'It was generally reported that something came on the Lord's Day night and pulled the clothes off his bed many times.'

There is nothing anonymous about the final ghost in this chapter, for she is perhaps the best known grey lady in the whole county. She is, of course, the ghost who haunts the old Hall at Burton Agnes on the A166, a few miles from Bridlington.

Burton Agnes Hall, the seat of the Boynton family, dates from about 1600 and was built by Sir Henry Griffiths. Old Sir Henry had three daughters and it is the youngest, Anne, who still haunts the Hall, 350 years after her death.

History records that Anne was attacked by footpads when returning from a visit to the home of the St Quintin family at Harpham. She was so badly injured that she died five days later. (At this point some historians disagree and say that the house itself was under attack by marauding thieves and Anne was mortally wounded in the struggle.) However, as she lay dying she asked her sisters to preserve her head at Burton Agnes Hall.

Despite their promises, this wish was not carried out and Anne was buried in the yard of the old Norman church at Burton Agnes. Not long afterwards were heard loud crashes, bangs and moans. Doors slammed and the disturbances became so frantic that the distracted family decided the girl's body should be disinterred. When the coffin was opened the head, already a grinning skull, was found to be severed from the shoulders, yet neither the limbs nor trunk showed any sign of putrefaction.

The skull was taken back to the house and for a time all

was quiet, until one day a servant girl threw it out of the window. It is said to have landed on a passing cart and the horses stopped, refusing to move an inch until it had been removed. Since then, all attempts to bury it in consecrated ground have led to all sorts of trouble. After being kept on a table in the great hall for many years, the skull was finally bricked up in a wall where it remains to this day, but Anne's ghost, known familiarly as 'Awd Nance', is still said to haunt the house she loved so much, apparently inspecting the furniture and making sure the house is kept up to standard.

CHAPTER 3

Knights of the High Toby

The great age of the highwayman was between the mid-seventeenth century and the early nineteenth century, a period of about 150 years. Although they were rife along the main roads, many in fact preferred the lonely roads and country lanes. It was to serve the stagecoaches that major highways like the Great North Road were built and they were to serve the purposes of the highwayman admirably. The Great North Road had an unsavoury reputation and people travelled it at their peril.

The ghosts that haunt this particular stretch of the Queen's Highway and the surrounding country lanes, are of men who were legends in their own lifetime and local folk have told terrifying tales ever since the highwaymen were a source of terror to travellers.

Dick Turpin, of course, lends his name to many of the old pubs and inns along this route and any room where Turpin and his contemporaries might possibly have hidden is almost certain to have a ghost story attached to it. His legendary exploits cover a wide area, but although his ghost has been seen on the A5 near Nuneaton and on the B488 at Woughton-on-the-Green near Bletchley, it has never been seen anywhere in Yorkshire. In fact legend has made far more of Dick Turpin than there really was. His greatest success was not as a highwayman but as a cattle stealer, near his father's home in Essex, and he was hanged, not for highway robbery, but for stealing a horse. However, be that as it may, any spectral horseman seen on the A1 since has been dubbed 'Dick Turpin'.

More authentic are the stories of the highwayman's ghost to be seen at various points between Scotch Corner and Boroughbridge, about six miles south east of Ripon. This ghost is without doubt that of Tom Hoggett, self-styled 'King of the High Tobeymen of the Great North Road'.

Hoggett was a real dyed-in-the-wool villain whose success in lifting purses over a wide area earned him quite a reputation. He was eventually caught by troopers sent out from York, at the Salutation Inn one stormy, moonless night and kept under guard until he could be taken to York on the mail coach the following day. The ever resourceful Hoggett bided his time and during the early hours of the morning was able to escape from his captors. He made a dash for the nearby River Swale, hoping to cross it at Langdon Fords, but in the darkness he stumbled into a pond and drowned. The pond still bears his name and it is said that no one who falls into it will survive.

Many stories are told of how, on moonless and stormy nights, Hoggett's ghostly figure can be seen, hatless and wearing a caped coat reaching to his ankles, gliding alongside the road at considerable speed, his coat glowing dimly, as if illuminated by a feeble lamp.

Further north at Ardwick-le-Street, a copse known as the 'Hanging Wood' was the favourite resort of another of Yorkshire's infamous sons, William Nevison. It was Nevison, not Turpin, who made the epic ride to York in 1678, covering the distance from London in the incredible time of fifteen hours and thirty-five minutes on the same black horse, the famous Black Bess. Despite this feat which was achieved to establish an alibi, Nevison was arrested and placed in York Castle, from where he managed to escape after bribing his jailer.

Charles II offered a reward of £20 for his recapture and it was not long before he was caught and subsequently hanged on the York Tyburn. His ghost is said to haunt the area around Batley, where in 1681 he was involved in a fight and killed a man called Darcy Fletcher.

A couple of miles north of Hornsea is the village of Atwick. Here an unknown headless highwayman has been seen on a number of occasions and at Hickleton near Goldthorpe, the ghost of an unknown highwayman terrified the author many years ago.

In those days I lived with my grandmother in Thurnscoe and worked at Doncaster, about eleven miles away. Because I didn't finish work until after 10.30 at night and the last bus left Doncaster at 9.30, I had to cycle home every night.

Leaving Doncaster, I would cycle up Barnsley Road through Scawsby and Marr and then begin a gradual uphill climb to Hickleton. Hickleton is neighboured by coal pits but it is an island of charm really, with a fine church at the crossroads and behind it, the seventeenth-century home of the Halifax family. Apart from that, several small cottages make up the remainder of the village.

On this particular night, as I cycled up the tree-lined road towards the church, I could see, between the trees on my left, the road which would cross my path outside the church. There was very little traffic along here in those days, but had anything been approaching the crossroads from my left, I would have been able to see it quite well. I was surprised to see a figure on horseback, trotting quite leisurely towards the junction. I remember thinking to myself, 'What a funny time for someone to be out on a horse,' for although it was late June and quite light, it was after 11.00 p.m.

The horseman came to the crossroads and stopped, looking down the road up which I was cycling, until suddenly the horse shied and I was able to distinguish quite clearly a billowing cape and tricorn hat. That in itself was bad enough, but then to my absolute terror both horse and rider vanished before my eyes. I was no more than fifty or sixty yards away by this time and I think it would be an understatement to say I was frightened, I was terrified. In fact, had I not been so near to home I would have turned back to Doncaster. As it was, I put my head down and pedalled furiously past the spot, covering the last two miles or so in record time.

Since then, while doing research for my books on ghosts, I have had one or two other frightening experiences, but I don't think I have ever been so terrified as I was that night in 1953.

When I reached home and had fully recovered, I told my grandmother of my experience, thinking she would accuse me of being over-imaginative, but she just listened quietly and then suggested I have a word with one of the neighbours who had been a policeman and used to patrol that area on his bike some years before.

The neighbour told me that he had seen the ghost himself on one occasion and that several people living in the village had reported seeing it, but no one knew who it was. One theory was that it was the ghost of a man ambushed by troops and killed on that spot. Research over the years has failed to bring any fresh evidence to light, but I understand the ghost has been seen as recently as 1977 by a lorry driver, who braked hard on reaching the crossroads, when a figure on a horse suddenly appeared from nowhere and vanished just as quickly.

On July 2nd, 1644, Cromwell defeated the Royalist army under Prince Rupert, at the battle of Marston Moor, just under a mile away from the village of Long Marston. Ever since that terrible day, tales of ghostly Cavaliers fighting it out with Roundheads have been told. Some people have claimed to have seen the battle silhouetted in the sky, while others tell of seeing ghostly survivors of this memorable clash, trudging by the wayside.

Back in November 1932, two touring motorists, lost in their search for the Wetherby road, found themselves travelling along the A59 which runs through the site of the old battlefield. Ahead of them they noticed a small group of perhaps three or four ragged individuals, stumbling silently along the ditch. Realizing there was something odd about them, they slowed down to look more closely. The figures were dressed as Cavaliers, with wide-brimmed hats turned up and fastened with cockades and long, flowing locks. At first they thought they must be actors from some carnival event.

The figures, moving in the same direction as the car, with their backs to it, suddenly staggered to the centre of the road and into the path of a bus approaching in the opposite direction. It was obvious that the driver of the bus could not see them as he did not even slow down and appeared to the two observers to drive straight through them. They stopped the car and searched the road on either side, but were unable to find a trace of anyone.

Today one still hears of solitary figures haunting the battleground. As a point of interest, the Old Hall at Long Marston which was used by Cromwell at the time of the battle of Marston Moor, is said to be haunted by his ghost.

A ghostly army was said to march through the Forest of Knaresborough and last century three farmers swore to seeing men clad in white, led by a commander in a scarlet tunic, their swords flashing in the sunlight.

Four miles north east of York, at Stockton-in-the-Forest, divisions of a large army were seen silhouetted in the sky, and a group of Roman soldiers who appeared to be lost were once seen marching through the walls of the Treasurer's House in York, some time in the 1950s.

The A64 between Pickering and York is haunted by a spectre called Nance, whose sole aim appears to be to help travellers in distress.

Nance, who was a farmer's daughter, came from Sheriff Hutton and was engaged to be married to a mailcoach driver on the York–Berwick run. In the case of Nance, however, absence failed to make the heart grow fonder and she found solace in the arms of another, eventually running off with him.

About a year later, the coachman was shocked to see Nance waiting at the side of the road, with a baby in her arms. She was so weak and ill, she could hardly stand. Stopping the coach he lifted her and the baby on to the seat beside him and as they continued their journey to York, the poor girl told him what had happened to her over the past year. It appears that the lover had abandoned her when the child was born. He was not only a married man, but a highwayman to boot.

The coachman took Nance and her child to the Black Swan Inn which used to stand in Coney Street, York, but both she and the baby died the same night from exhaustion and starvation.

Some years later, the coachman was again approaching York when he ran into dense fog, forcing him to take a postilion to lead the horses at snail's pace. Suddenly, the reins were jerked into the air by invisible hands and the horses set off at a frantic gallop. Looking round in terror, he saw Nance seated beside him, whipping the horses on, dressed as she had been on the night she died. She drove the horses flat out to York and into the yard of the Black Swan.

Nance can still be found on the A64, particularly on foggy nights, a lithe, young ragged girl, moving swiftly in the glare of the headlights. Any driver who cares to trust her can be confident that for as long as he can see her, he is safe. She will glide faster when the road is clear and will slow down should hidden dangers be ahead. The cat's eyes in the centre of the road will gleam clear through her body.

Drive along a certain street in Scarborough and you may come across the ghost of Lydia Bell, walking in the pink gown she wore on the night of her death. Lydia was the daughter of a well-known York confectioner who was found strangled on the beach at Scarborough in 1804. The street where she and her parents stayed on that fateful holiday has been haunted ever since. Also, while driving through the town, keep a lookout for the Black Horse of Scarborough, which has haunted the town for almost 800 years. Back in the twelfth century, reports of a black horse being seen galloping near to the town were made to the authorities. Over the centuries hundreds of people have claimed to have seen it and their accounts haven't varied much. A black, riderless horse passes, the sky suddenly goes black and there is a violent thunderstorm accompanied by hailstones.

At Sutton a ghost can be seen, said to be the spectre of Tom Busby, who was hanged and gibbeted in 1702 for killing his father-in-law. The story behind this ghost is that Tom married the daughter of a counterfeiter called Daniel Auty and, after the wedding, became Daniel's partner-in-crime. One day during an argument over how the money should be shared, Tom lost his temper and beat Auty to death with a hammer. The gallows where his body was left to rot stood opposite the Busby Stoop Inn and it is at this spot a figure has often been seen, with lolling head and a knotted rope still around his throat.

Another ghost, which has terrified many a lonely traveller, is that of the wicked Lord Wharton, which can be found on the A685 near Kirkby Stephen.

As Lord of the Manor, Lord Wharton presided at the peculiar Court of Ravenstonedale, a position which allowed him to exact extreme penalties. His list of crimes against tenants and wrongdoers makes even Stalin fade into insignificance. No one was in the least surprised when retribution struck, suddenly, in the form of blindness as he rode home alone.

When he died his ghost groped its way, with outstretched hands, along the same road.

The Yorkshire Moors provide a number of ghosts which the wary driver should look out for. For instance, the ghost of Kitty Garthwaite can be seen on the moors near Gilla-moor. Kitty, a local girl, was courting a boy from the nearby village of Hutton-le-Hole. When she became pregnant by him he deserted her and in despair she drowned herself in the River Dove one Sunday evening in 1784. Some days later her ex-lover was found dead in the same place and it was not long before local people reported seeing Kitty's ghost, sitting naked under the tree where she and her boyfriend used to meet. Needless to say, it was always the local men who saw her and many of them were lured to a watery grave.

Another moorland ghost is said to be that of Emily Brontë who haunts the stark windblown moors near Top Withens farm, thought to be the scene of her most successful novel *Wuthering Heights*. She can be seen in broad daylight, walking alone along the narrow path which leads to the Brontë Waterfall, a small fall about two miles from where she was brought up at the parsonage at Haworth, and which was a favourite spot for her and her sisters within sight of Top Withens.

Legend tells us of a tragic ghost which can be encountered

in the streets of Swinton, near Mexborough. Many years ago, there lived in the town a farmer, and his wife Mary. Mary was a good wife who took good care of her husband, despite the fact that he spent most of their hard-earned money on drink, afterwards coming home roaring drunk and very often beating the daylights out of the poor woman.

One night the farmer came home, drunk as usual, and demanded that Mary make him a good supper. The poor wretched woman was beside herself as there was no food and not a penny in the house with which to buy any. She decided her only salvation lay in slaughtering one of the two pigs they kept. Now the farmer loved one of these pigs, probably more than he loved Mary, and it was unfortunate for her that this was the one she should choose to kill. The farmer was furious and in his rage he picked up a large knife and chased her out of the house. Blind with fear she stumbled into the River Don nearby and drowned. Every year since then, she is said to ride through the streets of Swinton on the back of the wild boar, both of them screaming in terror.

Yorkshire also has its fair share of phantom coaches which are quite often witnessed on the county highways. A spectral coach driven by six horses is said to have been seen racing down a fellside in upper Wensleydale, and a coach and four has been seen on the old road leading from Settle to North Craven.

At Beverley, a ghostly coach and four, reportedly driven by the ghost of old Sir Percy, son of the 4th Earl of Northumberland, has been seen racing ever onward to eternity. Some people claim the horses are black and headless and the carriage contains a solitary passenger, a skeleton.

A further spectral carriage can be seen at Aislaby Hall,

near Whitby, while in the same town, yet another might be glimpsed careering along the road near the cliffs over which it plunges on reaching a certain point. Also in Whitby, in the area around Prospect Hill, has been seen the ghost of a man strolling along a path, carrying his head under his arm.

Although to my knowledge they have never been seen, spectral horses can be heard galloping in the dell near the cricket pitch at Bramham Park in North Yorkshire. They are thought to be the ghostly echoes of those who fled from the Battle of Bramham Moor in 1408.

Middleham Moor is said to be haunted by a woman wearing mourning clothes. Legend has it that in life she had two suitors and her plans to elope with one were discovered by the other who, in a jealous rage, murdered her on Middleham Moor. In the last century, the skeleton of a woman dressed in the remains of a black dress, was discovered high on the moor by peat diggers.

Another 'Lady in Black' can be met at Woodhall. Apart from her black clothes, she wears white gloves and carries a walking stick. She can be seen at any time of the year, day or night, and I am told that apart from her clothing she looks as normal and as solid as the trees around her.

Recently, after investigating an alleged haunted site near Wennington, I drove home rather late in the evening by way of Giggleswick and then the B6478 to Gisburn, where I would join the A682 to Nelson. Leaving the village of Wigglesworth I spotted a signpost for Tosside, which brought to mind a ghost I'd heard of and which I fervently hoped never to meet. This is the ghost of a young girl who lurks around the Tosside area and has been held responsible for causing numerous accidents.

According to local legend, many years ago, on a dark snowy morning, a young servant girl who had been sent to fetch water from the stream, fell in and drowned. It is claimed that this is the ghost that lies in wait for a motor car to approach and then runs directly into its path, causing the motorist to swerve violently, usually ending up in the ditch.

Another spectre associated with water is that of a woman who haunts the banks of the River Ouse near Beningbrough, about eight miles from York. She was said to have been murdered here in the late seventeenth century. She was the housekeeper to the family at Beningbrough Hall who, it is said, spurned the advances of the steward of the estate. Because of this, he paid a local poacher, William Vasey, to murder her. Vasey was caught and hanged at York, but the housekeeper's ghost still haunts the spot where she met her end, presumably from drowning.

The anonymous ghost of a woman can be seen at Lady Well in Melsonby, up in North Yorkshire. Little is known about her, except that she is minus a head.

Should the reader be in Skipton and see the ghost of Lady Anne Clifford riding up the main street in her spectral coach towards the castle gateway, then he can expect to hear within days, of the death of the Lord of the Honour of Skipton.

Mrs M. Hall of Fartown, Huddersfield, is convinced that she and her mother had a close encounter of the spectral kind when returning from a visit to New House Hall in the latter part of 1936.

She told me: 'We were walking home arm-in-arm up Wiggan Lane, which in those days was lit by a solitary gas lamp. There was a full moon and I remember it was a crisp, clear night.' About halfway up the lane they suddenly saw a young woman dressed in white and wearing what appeared to be some kind of veil on her head, which flowed out behind her. She seemed to float across the road in front of them, through a stone wall and disappeared into the field beside the road. Mrs Hall said, 'We took a tighter grip on each other and, picking up courage, looked over the wall into the field, but there was no one there. I firmly believe we had seen the ghost of the young woman who is said to haunt the Hall.'

A similar experience happened to Mrs Adele Lathom of Batley a few years ago. She was returning home by car from the cinema at Leeds with three friends when they lost their way. Two of the friends were asleep in the back seat and Adele was sitting in the front with Mandy, the driver. Suddenly, ahead of them they noticed what appeared to be white steam in the centre of the road. She told me, 'At first I thought it was either a collection of steam from some factory or other, or else a large polythene bag. But as the car approached, it appeared to rise and float up over the top, silently. I was terrified and for no reason at all I felt tears rolling down my cheeks.' She noticed that Mandy's cheeks were also wet with tears. Neither of them could understand why they were crying, nor could they fathom out what the shape was.

'The following day,' she continued, 'we were told at work that the mother of one of our friends had died at about the time we saw the object on the Beeston—Cottingley road. We were even more astounded to learn that at the time we saw the apparition, for that is what it was, we were passing the crematorium where she was to be cremated later in the week.'

As Mrs Agnes Kelly of Fartown, Huddersfield, drove her car into a sharp bend, the glare of oncoming headlights picked out the figure of a young, fair-haired boy. Horrified, she swung the steering wheel over as the boy's freckled face loomed up in front of the windscreen. That single act probably saved her life. She crashed into a parked car, but suffered only shock. As she waited for an ambulance, she anxiously asked a policeman, 'Have I killed the boy?' But there was no boy.

A court heard, in January 1981, that what Mrs Kelly saw as she took the bend in Somerset Road, Huddersfield, was a vision of an eight-year-old child, who had been knocked down and killed by a car on the same spot many years before. After the case she said, 'But for that vision I am sure I would have driven straight into the car coming up the hill towards me. I most probably would have been killed.'

Finally, the story of a ghost that appeared to be so natural at the time that the young man who was witness to it still cannot believe that what he saw was a ghost.

Back in the mid-1930s young Robert was cycling home from school along Dewsbury Road, Leeds, and approached the traffic lights at the crossing near Meadow Lane. As the lights were against him, he pulled up behind a tramcar and, as he did so, happened to glance across to the other side of the road where he saw his grandfather approaching from the opposite direction. The lights changed and Robert pulled away behind the tram and, as he passed his grandfather, called out to him, 'Hello Grandad.'

The old man raised his walking stick in acknowledgement and, smiling, waved back at him. Robert was quite used to seeing his grandfather at this particular stretch of Dewsbury Road once or twice each week, because the old man used to visit a friend of his who ran a tobacconist shop there, buy his tobacco and stop for a while to catch up on the latest gossip. Robert rode on home, trying to catch up with the tramcar, so he didn't bother to look around again and, so far as he knew, his grandfather carried on towards the shop.

When he got home, Robert put his bike in the back yard, washed his hands and set about ravenously eating his tea, as all schoolboys do, pausing only to mention quite casually to his parents, that he had seen his grandfather in Dewsbury Road. His parents stopped eating and looked at each other in silence for a moment or two, before his mother said quietly, 'Your Grandad died, late last night.'

Robert was to say many times later, 'There was no mistake. I could have recognized him anywhere. His distinguished appearance, waxed moustache and walking stick. I know it was my grandad that I saw and that he recognized and acknowledged me.'

CHAPTER 4

Things That Go 'Bump'

Most people tend to think that ghosts only haunt rambling old houses. I would agree that the atmosphere of some of these old places is often conducive to imaginative sightings, but it is quite misleading to think ghosts cannot haunt a modern home, because in my experience many truly authenticated ghost stories come from such places. As I said in *Lancashire's Ghosts and Legends*, my own home, built in 1904, is comparatively modern and is haunted by a delightful Edwardian of a most likeable disposition, who exists quite happily side-by-side with my down-to-earth family. Unfortunately, other people are not always quite so lucky.

Miss Joy Bailey had two rather unnerving experiences: the first, in 1971, was when she lived with her parents in an old terraced house in Masbrough, near Rotherham. Going to bed as usual one evening, leaving her parents to sleep downstairs as they often did in the cold weather, she snuggled down into her warm bed and quickly fell asleep. Miss Bailey said, 'At about 3 o'clock in the morning, I awoke for no reason at all and was surprised to hear footsteps crossing my parents' room and then go down the stairs.' Thinking that perhaps one of her parents had been taken ill, she called out, but there was no reply. Plucking up courage, she hopped out of bed and went downstairs to see if all was well. Both her parents were fast asleep. She continued, 'I woke my father and told him about the footsteps and he, thinking it might be a burglar, searched the house thoroughly. All the doors were bolted still and there were no signs of any disturbance.'

Miss Bailey said that she always had the feeling that someone was watching her whenever she went into the small bedroom. Her mother agreed there was something about the house which she could not quite understand and that she too had been surprised to hear footsteps about the house when she had been sitting alone at night.

The second incident occurred in a house in Scrooby Street at Greasbrough, on a hot Saturday afternoon during the summer of 1978. At the time the house was empty as it was undergoing extensive alterations and Miss Bailey, out of curiosity, decided to have a look around to see how the alterations were coming along. She said, 'As soon as I entered the house I could sense something was wrong. It is very hard to describe the feeling which came over me, but I should say it was a mixture of fear and sadness; and cold, intense cold.'

Reaching the top of the stairs she went to look at the bathroom, but these feelings became so intense she froze at the doorway, unable to open the door. She decided to get out of the house as quickly as possible.

Later, she happened to mention to her mother that she had been looking over the house, but took care not to mention her experience. Her mother, to her surprise, told her that she remembered how, during the Second World War, a woman who lived at the house had been accidentally electrocuted in the bathroom.

A more distinctive, but none-the-less frightening spectre, made life intolerable for Mrs Frances Mills and her parents when, as a young girl, she lived with them at Allinson's Cottages in Mexborough. The cottages have now been demolished, but they stood on what was known as Cross-gates.

Mrs Mills told me: 'My parents had been troubled by this

spectre for some length of time and I saw it at least three times. My father worked the night-shift at the local colliery and therefore each afternoon he would go to bed. Many times he rushed downstairs to see which of us children had been clomping up and down them, when all the time we had been playing quietly in the back room.'

Once, while her grandmother was staying with them and sleeping with the children, they all felt something pass over the foot of the bed. Likewise, when an aunt stayed with them, she was making the bed in this same room, when something touched her on the shoulder. 'Needless to say,' said Mrs Mills, 'she didn't stay much longer after that.'

The first time Mrs Mills actually saw the ghost she saw only part of a face peering round the top of the stairs into her bedroom. She had been sent to bed for some minor incident, but she soon started shouting out in fear, bringing the rest of the household quickly up the stairs to see what was wrong.

Twice in later years she saw the figure again, quite plainly. It was the figure of a man. 'In those days we slept in an old iron bed with old-fashioned brass bedsteads, which are much in demand today,' she said. 'I woke up one night and saw the figure of a man quite plainly. Actually I thought I was dreaming and put my head under the bed-clothes, but when I peeped out again he was still there.' The figure was not very tall, in fact his head just cleared the bottom rail. He had a long nose which was quite noticeable on such a short man; and he appeared to be wearing a night shirt, or possibly a shroud. The figure stood motionless, pointing into the corner to the right of the bed.

Mrs Mills's mother awoke one morning to see a blue light dancing from side to side in the wardrobe mirror. She got out of bed and opened the bedroom curtains, but there was nothing to account for it. No amount of investigation could account for the hauntings, but it is believed the figure may have some connection with the two men who were the previous occupiers of the cottage.

Mr W.D. Mather of Sheffield related a similar phenomenon, although at the time he did not recognize it as such. It was some time between 1908 and 1910 and Mr Mather was living with his family in a Victorian house which contained the old-fashioned system of bells. These had to be pulled manually, a series of wires from each of which went up through the attic and back down to the kitchen, where a set of eight or nine iron clappers were attached to the wall just below the ceiling.

He said, 'One evening, the family were all sitting around the kitchen fire, when all the bells began to ring at once and continued to do so for several minutes.' His father explored the house from cellar to attic, but was unable to trace either a human or an animal which might have tampered with the wires. Mr Mather continued, 'As we had an aunt staying with us at that time, who had come over from her home in Paris to visit us, the whole incident was dismissed as a welcome peal to her, on her return to her native city.'

This incident made a profound impression on Mr Mather which has never left him, although the idea of the supernatural would have been ridiculed by his parents, who were very Victorian and would not admit to there being such 'unholy' things as ghosts.

Mrs Jeanne Shackleton, of Huddersfield, had a rather unnerving experience during the Second World War. At that time she was in her early twenties and living in an older-type terraced house. She told me: 'There was a passage between my house and the house next door, with the staircase on the farther wall and so, when I heard footsteps in the early hours of the morning, I knew they just had to be on my staircase.'

The footsteps stopped just outside her bedroom door. Thinking it was an intruder and worried about the safety of the children asleep in the next room, Mrs Shackleton got up and taking a large, heavy naval torch went to investigate. There was no one on the stairs, the children were safely asleep and after going through the whole house, checking the doors and windows and finding nothing, she went back to bed rather puzzled.

She continued: 'I lay in bed listening and a short time later, I heard the same footsteps again and began to count them. There was one step that always creaked when anyone came up the stairs, so I knew just how far the footsteps had come when I heard it creak. They really were on my staircase and again they stopped outside my bedroom door.' This time she was too afraid to check again and lay in a state of fear for the remainder of the night.

The next morning a very worried Jeanne Shackleton discussed the previous night's events at her mother's home. She learned that before she took the house, it had been occupied by two elderly spinsters and their brother. One night the brother hanged himself from a hook in the kitchen and shortly afterwards the sisters had moved out.

Someone suggested that the next time Mrs Shackleton heard the footsteps, she should open the bedroom door boldly and demand to know who or what was bothering her. She went on to say, 'When I next heard them I was all for doing what had been suggested, but I was young then and if the spectre of the man was to appear looking all horrible and with his neck all twisted, I'm sure I would have died — of fright. So, to my eternal regret, I never opened the door to ask what was, I suppose, a vital question.'

A similar, but rather more sinister experience befell Mrs Bould of Wakefield, a number of years ago. Mrs Bould told me: 'I hadn't been married long and my husband and I lived in an old house in the middle of Tavern Street, which was situated in Kirkgate. My husband was in the habit of going out with his pals most nights, leaving me at home with our little girl.'

The night in question was a Monday. The little girl was in bed with measles and, as usual, Mrs Bould was alone downstairs. Being Monday, it was, as it has been for generations of Yorkshire Mondays, washday; and she was tidying up after putting the clothes ready for ironing. She continued: 'There was no gas or electricity in the house. I took a candle and went upstairs to see if my daughter was all right. Having satisfied myself, I crept quietly down the stairs carrying the lighted candle in front of me.'

Nearing the bottom of the stairs, a figure, which she describes as 'black shrouded', came through the living-room door and appeared to glide through the wall into the pantry. Mrs Bould said the figure was that of a man wearing a black, hooded cloak of some kind, with his arms folded inside the cloak. She said, 'I let out a shout thinking my husband had come home early and was playing a trick on me. I went to the pantry intending to tell him just what I thought of him — but the pantry was empty. Needless to say, I went outside and stood at the garden gate until I saw my husband coming up the street.' There is no apparent explanation for this ghostly visitation and it was not very long afterwards that Mr and Mrs Bould moved to another house.

A more recent haunting was experienced by Mrs A.K. Vaughan-Morris of Featherstone in March and April 1980, which is all the more remarkable because she has seen the ghost in two different places, her daughter's home and her own.

During the Christmas holidays, Mrs Vaughan-Morris

was staying at her daughter's, sharing a top-floor bedroom with her little grandson. She awoke one night feeling cold and was surprised to see a little figure walking towards her. It was a girl of about seven or eight, wearing a long dress and pinafore, with golden curly hair and holding an old-fashioned stool in front of her. At first she thought it was one of the grandchildren out of bed, until the figure came closer to the bed and suddenly disappeared.

The matter was forgotten and Mrs Vaughan-Morris returned to her own home where, she says, the little girl again materialized on January 6th, 1980, beside her bed, dressed as before, but this time she was minus the stool. After this things began to happen regularly, as follows:

March 5th: A man's figure appeared and just as suddenly disappeared, following which a bouquet of flowers fell on to the bed and disappeared also. Mrs Vaughan-Morris fell asleep, but later in the night awoke feeling cold. She was astonished to see a baby's arm, clad in a blue sleeve, with frilled cuff and the little hand held out towards her. It disappeared towards the door.

March 14th: Woke up with a shivery feeling around the face and saw what appeared to be a basket floating towards her face, only to vanish after a few seconds.

March 19th: Again, Mrs Vaughan-Morris woke up shivering and feeling that someone was leaning over her. The basket shape reappeared accompanied by what can only be described as a folded bolt of cloth of varying colours. It appeared to fall off the bed and when she reached over to pick it up, again there was nothing to be seen.

March 21st: The basket appeared again. Mrs Vaughan-Morris cried out, 'Go away. I don't like you.' At which the basket appeared to float away sideways, before disappearing.

These and similar related incidents continue right up to the present day. Mrs Vaughan-Morris wrote to me on April 11th, 1980, following a further night of interrupted sleep. That night she had awakened to find the basket, filled up with what appeared to be twigs, resting on her chest. She reached out to touch it, but as before, there was nothing there. Each time these incidents occur the room temperature drops rapidly, her face feels icy and she is conscious of somebody nearby.

Mrs Vaughan-Morris wonders whether the child might have any connection with her grand-daughter, who was born prematurely on October 1st, 1970 and died five hours later. On February 19th, 1977, her husband died suddenly. As they were very close, it could well be that because of her present heart condition, he is worried about her health. There seems to be no other explanation.

Fifty years ago, when Mrs J. Halstead of Sowerby Bridge was a child, she experienced something which she has remembered ever since. She told me: 'My mother was in hospital and father had washed my sister and me and told us to sit by the fire in the large wicker chair, whilst he and my brother made the beds. Suddenly, my sister, who was two years older than me, whispered to me not to make a noise. In a terrified whisper she told me to look under the table.' Looking through the back of the chair, Mrs Halstead could see a large, white, filmy shape, not actually a man or a woman, but more a vague outline. She said, 'I was not in the least scared. As "it" drifted towards the cellar door, I said to my sister, "Don't be frightened, Mary. It's only a ghost!" At this Mary screamed and rushed to the bedroom door. She had frightened me by this act and I rushed after her, screaming too.'

Many years later, the girl's father told them that often he

heard noises during the night. Thinking one of the girls might be sleepwalking, he would take a candle and go downstairs, only to find that the noise was caused by the old rocking chair, gently rocking on its own in the corner.

Mrs L. Hagell of Leeds had a similar childhood experience when, at the age of four, she lived at Goring House, near Wakefield.

She says that as far as she can remember, the man who built the house was so disappointed with the finished result that he hanged himself. She told me: 'I think I remember someone saying he had hanged himself from the banister in the hall, but my sister says he hanged himself in the cellar.' Whichever way it was, he was considered to be the cause of the strange night-time noises, sounding as if he was tapping his way across the hall with his stick, on what sounded like a parquet floor. No shade was ever witnessed so far as I can make out, but doors were often seen to open and close on their own accord.

Mr John Harris of Halifax related to me a number of incidents which took place in 1962, when he lived in an old house in Southowram.

Mr Harris had married in 1958 during his National Service days, but it was not until 1960 that he spent much time in the house, except during his short periods of leave. However, in February 1962, following demob, his wife went into hospital to have a baby. Mr Harris said, 'I decided to take the opportunity to do a few home improvements while my wife was in hospital. At the time I was working the 2 p.m. to 10 p.m. shift, so when I started putting some shelves up on this particular night, it must have been after 11 p.m. Because of the thickness of the walls, I knew it would not disturb the neighbours.'

Having finished the shelves in the small hours, Mr Harris

decided to shampoo the living-room carpet and banked up the fire, in order that it would dry reasonably quickly. He continued: 'I had no idea of the time, but it must have been in the early hours of the morning. The fire was roaring and the carpet was drying nicely. The old cat was curled up on the hearth and I sat by the fire to have a mug of tea, feeling highly pleased with my night's work.'

Suddenly there was a resounding crash, rather like a heavy door slamming shut. The cat leapt up and appeared to fly around the room several inches from the ground, howling in terror. 'I thought someone had come in at the front door and had slammed it behind them, but when I went to look there was no one about and the door was still bolted. I unlocked it and looked outside — nothing, but the cat shot out of the house and disappeared up the hillside, where it remained for several days.'

Returning to the living room rather puzzled, Mr Harris suddenly became aware of what he could only describe as 'giant footsteps' crossing the room overhead, from one corner to the other, slowly and very loud. Breaking into a cold sweat, he forced himself to go up to the bedroom and investigate, but he found nothing.

The following morning he called on a neighbour in the hope of finding some explanation, but the woman replied that if he intended staying in the house he would have to get used to the strange noises, for she too had heard them quite often, over the years.

There are two possible explanations for the mysterious events that took place in this house. At some time previously, a firm of builders had done some excavating on the land behind the house and they had unearthed a plague pit, containing a number of skeletons and thought to go back to Cromwellian times, for it is understood that Cromwell camped at Southowram to avoid the Halifax plague. Could they have disturbed some spirit from these times? Perhaps, but the second theory seems to me nearer the mark and Mr Harris also subscribes to it.

Mr Harris discovered in a tattered old book about the area that the original buildings were known as 'Blaithe Rood' and had been in turn a monastery, a plague house and a farm (Blaithroyd Farm). They were then converted into five separate dwellings. The author described how he had in fact visited Blaithe Rood and had been very impressed, not only by the magnificent stone fireplace at one end of the hall, but also by the stained-glass windows at the opposite end, which depicted a one-legged man. 'This,' said Mr Harris, 'could explain the peculiar walk which, on reflection, could have been of a person with a limp or an artificial leg. This would explain why the footsteps were heavy and well spaced, but who the one-legged man was, I have not been able to discover.'

Mr Albert Paradise has lived in Stainland, Halifax, for sixty-three years. Before moving to his present address a few years ago, he had lived with his father, until his death, in a cottage a few hundred yards down the road. Mr Paradise told me: 'The building was erected in 1705 and we ourselves moved in about 1920. My father had a fear of gas and electricity, considering it to be highly dangerous and so, from 1920 up until after his death in the late 1950s, we survived with nothing more than a coal fire for cooking on and oil lamps and candles for lighting.'

In all the thirty-odd years he and his father had lived in the cottage, they had never seen or heard anything, but after his father's death a number of mysterious events took place, culminating in one particular incident which, Mr Paradise said, 'frightened me half to death'.

It was New Year's Eve, 1956. Because he didn't have electricity in the house, he used to go to bed reasonably early and listen to an old accumulator-operated radio set.

He did not drink and in fact still doesn't, so cannot be accused of having been celebrating the New Year. He said, 'Because it was a moonlit night, I left the bedroom curtains open and lay in bed fully awake, listening to some classical music on the radio. The bed was facing the fireplace and over the mantelpiece was a picture, which was quite old. Suddenly, a face seemed to appear in the frame in place of the picture and then, to my absolute terror, a figure appeared, as if walking out of the fireplace from the house next door, which floated towards the bottom of the bed. His face was a ghastly white. He had sunken eyes and long, flowing hair, which was as white as his face.' The figure appeared to be playing a violin, his head moving from side to side, long hair shaking as if in time to the radio. Mr Paradise admits to racing from the room in sheer terror.

A couple of nights later, he was making his supper in the kitchen when he got a distinct feeling that someone was standing behind him. Too afraid to turn around, he shouted, 'Oh, not tonight. Go away, please.' He tells me he sat in the kitchen all night, too afraid to go to bed. There does not appear to be any record of other incidents in the house prior to these and I am told that once the fireplace had been bricked up and electricity was installed, there were no further incidents.

The bed-time antics of a sexy spectre frightened a young mother of four towards the end of November, 1980. She became so upset she called the local vicar to bless her house in a bid to be rid of the saucy spook.

Mr and Mrs Ken Batty and their family had been haunted by a series of eerie happenings since they moved into their council home at Thurcroft, near Rotherham, early in 1980. But it was the incidents of November of that year that were the most unnerving. Mrs Batty said, 'I was in bed one morning when I felt the blanket being pulled down from my chin. Then I felt my chin being tickled and I naturally thought it was my husband back from work — I was pleasantly surprised, but when I looked up, there was a weird face with staring eyes and no teeth, grinning at me. When I screamed, it suddenly vanished.'

Previous incidents in the Batty household had involved cups being hurled across the kitchen, lampshades vibrating violently and the sound of footsteps when there was no one else in the house.

No one can shed any light on the identity of the spectre, or why it should suddenly turn up as, so far as I can ascertain, it has never troubled any previous tenants. The local suggestion is that this is the ghost of an old retired collier, who lived in the house some years ago, but as no one else has yet seen it, this can only be pure speculation. One thing is certain though, Mrs Batty knows she was not imagining things.

About nine years ago Mrs E. Parker of Brighouse moved with her husband into a house which had been converted from an old pub, the Black Bull at the top of Elland Edge. She told me: 'On going into the house for the first time I was immediately aware of a very strange and frightening atmosphere. I stood in the hall at the bottom of the wrought-iron staircase and for no reason at all, called out, "You're welcome to stay if you don't frighten me." Why I said it still puzzles me, but I knew somehow that the place had a ghost.'

On their very first night there, they were disturbed by footsteps. Her husband, who was a farmer and as down-to-earth as they come, felt sure that someone had broken in so he got up to investigate, without success. Time after time, night after night, the footsteps could be heard, clomping all over the house.

Mrs Parker continued: 'I was always the last to go to bed

and one night I was annoyed by a curious tapping which seemed to come from the wall beside my chair. This went on for several nights, sometimes being so continuous as to drive me to bed. Other times I would tap back, only to receive an answering tap.'

Some time later, Mrs Parker says she had a vivid dream which she still remembers quite clearly, in which a fair-haired lady in a blue dress came into the bedroom and beckoned for her to follow her into one of the cellars. Here the woman pointed to a loose stone in the wall and indicated to Mrs Parker that she should remove it. She said, 'The dream was so vivid. The next day I realized that the part of the cellar I had dreamed about was immediately beneath where I heard the tapping most nights.'

A couple of days later, she could stand the strain no longer and told her husband of her experiences and her dream. She was convinced there was something in the cellars, but for some reason had always been afraid to go down there. Her husband said there was no harm in looking, particularly if it would give her peace of mind. He went down, put on the light and then called to her to come and show him where the woman had been pointing. She said, 'It was uncanny. It was exactly as I had seen it in my dream, loose stone and all. There was nothing behind the loose stone except an empty cavity, but after that day when we left the stone in the middle of the cellar floor, I was never bothered again by the tapping. The thing is though, did I let some force loose into the house, for often after that I heard footsteps down there, and my dogs wouldn't stay in the house at all during the night and would often be seen jumping and growling at something I couldn't see, at the cellar head.'

Other, stranger things began to be experienced by both Mrs Parker and her husband. One morning she was feeling a little out of sorts and stayed in bed rather later than usual.

Suddenly she heard footsteps coming up the stairs. Thinking it was her husband coming to scold her for lying in, she turned her face to the wall and pretended to be asleep. The footsteps stopped beside the bed and she heard a pitying voice saying, 'Oh dear,' following which the footsteps went back down the stairs. Mrs Parker said, 'I shouted out "What time is it?" but there was no reply. I then thought to myself, "Funny, him pitying me." Anyway, I got up and went downstairs only to find the house empty.'

It had not been her husband. She discovered later that he had not been back to the house all morning, as on that particular day he too had been late up and was behind with the milking. However the most amazing part of the story is yet to come. I will let Mrs Parker tell it in her own words, exactly as she told it to me.

'It was after that I felt some sort of affinity with the ghost. "He" had pity for me, something my husband never had. So when I was upset I used to go to the staircase and cry on it and somehow seemed to draw comfort. So, the footsteps continued outside my room and I felt safe. Then, one day came the realization that I couldn't continue like this and I had to get away from the house as soon as possible. A friend came to the house some weeks later to tell me I had got another house and as he stood at the kitchen door telling me this, a coat hanger came flying through the room and hit him on the head. It was as if the ghosts or whatever didn't want me to go.'

The reader may find this story difficult to believe, but there are many witnesses to these happenings up at the old house, who are prepared to swear to the events described here.

Swinsty Hall, at Timble, is well over four hundred years old and looks, from the outside at least, like the background location for a horror movie. Its present owners, Mr and Mrs Cuckston, have lived here for the past thirteen years and during that time they have had several experiences of the paranormal and although the ghosts have never been seen, their presence is both heard and felt.

The first incident took place about a year after the Cuckstons had moved into Swinsty Hall. Mrs Cuckston was in the basement kitchen, when she heard someone call, 'Hello.' She says she was quite alone in the house, except for her young daughter who was quietly eating her dinner. Mrs Cuckston shouted back, to let the person know where in this large house she could be found; and at the same time she started up the stairs to the door to see who was there. She was surprised to find no one.

Several weeks later, both she and her husband were in the kitchen, when suddenly her husband shouted, 'Hello?', as though in reply to someone shouting to him. Mrs Cuckston had not heard the voice herself, but watched her husband going through the same motions that she herself had done earlier.

Later, more bizarre and disturbing events occurred. The main bedroom, used by Mr and Mrs Cuckston, is spacious and dignified, with a stone fireplace. Many people will have been born and will have died in this room, over the centuries. Because of the layout of the room, the bed can only be placed in one of two positions and therefore, again, for over four hundred years previous occupiers will more than likely have sited their beds where the Cuckstons have theirs today.

One night, Mrs Cuckston had gone to bed some time before her husband Alan, who, as a music historian and harpsichord enthusiast, was listening to some music downstairs on the stereo. She was rather tired and ready for sleep. Some minutes later, whilst beginning to doze, she thought she heard her husband come upstairs and a few minutes later felt him climb into bed beside her, although, strangely, he didn't turn out the light. Mrs Cuckston fell asleep, but awoke after only a few minutes to find the bedroom light was still on and her husband was not in bed. In fact, he was still up and dressed and listening to his music downstairs.

In 1971, the Cuckstons' youngest daughter was born in the middle bedroom of the house, at 1 o'clock in the afternoon. During the remainder of the day, Mrs Cuckston slept quite a lot and the baby lay in the crib beside the bed. The room had been well prepared for the happy event and was warm and pleasant but, despite this, during the night Mrs Cuckston was awakened by a feeling of almost paralysing coldness. The bedclothes were still in place and she was unable to account for this eerie coldness. After a few moments she felt a warm blanket being placed over her. The sudden warmth was as comforting as the cold had been disturbing and she soon fell asleep again.

The following morning when Mrs Cuckston awoke, the room was warm and the baby was awake in the crib beside her. She later thanked her husband for bringing her an extra blanket during the cold night and was surprised when he told her that he had been exhausted and had slept soundly in the master bedroom, without once getting out of bed!

My final ghost in this chapter is that of a woman, described as being over six feet tall, who troubled a family in their corporation home at Meltham, Huddersfield, in 1961.

The ghost was first seen in the parents' bedroom on the night of Friday, March 31st. It was big and horrid, said the occupants. The figure was seen three more times during that Easter period, then again, in the middle of August of the same year. Mrs Horn, the wife of the occupier, was sleeping alone because her husband was working the night shift. She was terrified, especially as the ghost reached out, touching her face with hands that were like cold mist.

Mrs Horn's husband, Arnold, saw the ghost one Sunday night in October. He hit out at it and it appeared to back through the bedroom wall into the room where his six-year-old daughter was sleeping. Suddenly she screamed and came rushing out of the bedroom.

About a week later the ghost was seen by a neighbour and a youth. The parents then learned from their eight-year-old son that night after night the ghost had sat on his bed and spent some time talking to him and massaging his legs; he was not afraid of it. The couple had often heard the boy talking aloud in the night about what he had been doing at school, but they thought he had been talking in his sleep. Now they were not so sure.

A medium was called in and while the children slept, a seance was held in the parents' bedroom where the figure had first manifested itself. The medium claimed afterwards to have seen the distinct form of a woman aged about sixty, with her hair tied in a bun. She also claimed to have heard a voice whisper the name 'Annie' and had been subjected to a strong desire to open one of the drawers in the dressing table behind her, in which she believed a photograph of the spirit could be found.

The description fitted that of Arnold Horn's aunt Annie, who had died nine years previous to these events. It now appeared likely that the apparition of this relative had returned to help heal one of their children; for the boy to whom it constantly appeared had been stricken with meningitis when he was only two years old. Doctors had said he might never walk again. I understand that within two years of these events taking place, the boy managed to regain the full use of his legs and in a very short time, became a normal, healthy child.

Thanks to the healing spirit of great aunt Annie!

CHAPTER 5

The Haunts of The Drinking Man

Until fairly recently the village pub, like the church, was the focal point of the community. On winter evenings the locals would gather round the roaring fire, telling and re-telling the stories and legends of generations, or listening to the tales told by passing travellers. Perhaps it was the travellers themselves, who as victims of a leg-pull, brought away with them terrifying tales of apparitions, which are said to haunt some of our older watering places. No doubt some of the ghost stories told over a quiet drink were a mixture of fact and fantasy, but many of them were not, as some of these ghosts still rattle their chains from time to time, even today. The following stories are by no means exhaustive and whether or not the reader believes them, the establishments themselves are well worth a visit for the beverages alone.

The Bailey Club at Monk Bretton, near Barnsley, adjoins an old Quaker burial ground, which is thought to be the reason for some of the mysterious manifestations that have been witnessed in recent years. Members of staff have often seen the apparition of a man in an old Quaker-style hat, looking, as one told me, 'like yon chap on t'porridge packet.'

One manager working in his office late at night, looked up to see the figure swaying in the middle of the room, before disappearing. The temperature dropped rapidly and an icy blast swept the room. Another member of staff heard the concert-room door open and shivered as a gust of cold air preceded a dark figure, which glided past. However, the most amazing occurrence was when several members of staff together witnessed the club's organ being played by invisible hands, producing not 'punk rock' or the latest 'pop' tunes, but an old hymn!

The Crown Hotel at Askern, near Doncaster, has a room which is haunted and which frightened the life out of Mrs D. Banks of Pogmoor, Barnsley, some years ago.

She told me that when she was in her teens, her parents were the licensees of the Crown and she had a bedroom on the first floor, directly at the foot of the stairs leading to the second floor landing. The second floor consisted of bedrooms and a bathroom, and at the end of the corridor was what she describes as, 'The Room'.

She said, 'Although the other rooms on the second floor were in constant use with bed and breakfast clientele and had been for many years before we moved in, the room in question had not been used and by the look of it, it had never been opened in years.' The room was full of junk and dust covered everything. As she had such a small room on the first floor, Mrs Banks asked her mother if it could be cleaned out and made into a room for herself. She continued: 'My mother agreed and we set to work cleaning it out and decorating. Pleased with the finished result I moved my belongings into my new room, a room I might add, in which I was only to spend one night.'

That night, eagerly contemplating the delights of a larger, newly decorated bedroom, she went to bed happily and was soon asleep. Although she says she usually slept right through the night, and still does, on this particular night she was awakened by the strangest of feelings. Mrs Banks said, 'It may sound odd to say I was wakened by a feeling, as one is normally awakened by a sound. But there was no sound, only the strangest feeling of not being alone, of being watched. It was a most uneasy atmosphere.'

For some inexplicable reason she looked over towards the windows and the heavy drapes blocking out the light, when suddenly and without any warning the drapes began to open. She went on to say, 'I can see them now, slowly drawing across the window and flooding the room with moonlight. I can still hear them, the only sound in that strange atmosphere, the sound of the curtain runners on the rail, as they worked together to open the curtains.'

Who or what opened the curtains? Mrs Banks did not wait to find out. She fled in sheer panic, for as the room was filled with moonlight, she could see that she was still alone. In fact she spent the remainder of the night sitting on the bed in her old room, with the light on.

The following morning, her brother found her still sitting on the bed in her old room. She told him of her horrifying experience of the previous night and he asked whether, when she and her mother cleaned out the room, did they not consider it strange that the windows were barred, or that there was a large lock and several bolts on the *outside* of the door? He went on to say that many times, when using the bathroom next door to this particular bedroom, he had heard noises, rather like the sounds of furniture being moved about, although the room was, he knew, only full of junk.

The pub is over two hundred years old and although it has not been possible to find out who haunts it, one thing is certain: whoever or whatever was locked in that room, someone had tried to make sure it never got out.

Leaving Lancashire from Colne on the B6250 at Laneshaw Bridge, passing through what was once part of the forest of Trawden and over the Keighley Moors towards Haworth, one passes through the tiny village of Stanbury. Standing just outside the village on the right-hand side of the road, silent and lonely, is the Olde Silent Inn, a beautiful old inn, formerly known as The Eagle, but far better known as the place where, with a price on his head, Bonnie Prince Charlie was given shelter and food. One can still see the trapdoor through which the Young Pretender is said to have dropped on to the back of a conveniently placed horse to make good his escape, as his pursuers hammered at the door.

However, it is not the ghost of the young Charles Stuart which haunts this lovely old inn, but the soothing spectre of a previous landlady, a sweet and kindly old soul, who strokes the forehead of fitful sleepers. She was a lovely old dear who used to feed the many wild cats that once roamed these moors, calling them for their food by ringing a small bell. Folk in these parts say that she can still be heard at times, her little bell tinkling in the distance, soft and gentle like the sound of fairy bells being carried on a gentle breeze.

At Long Preston, the eighteenth-century coach house, the Boar's Head, has quite an interesting history. It was originally built as a stable for a local landowner, but was turned into a public house in 1752. In the great days of the stagecoach, the pub was a busy hostelry at the side of a toll road. It is interesting to note that the names of every landlord since 1752 are recorded on a plaque in the village.

Tradition has it that one of these men hanged himself in the hotel's beer cellar, and his ghost is said to haunt the building. There is an old photograph hanging in one corner of the bar. It shows an old woman, said to be the mother of the dead man. Legend says that providing the photograph hangs in the hotel 'for all time', it is believed the ghost will not return.

On January 5th, 1981, it was widely reported in the press that landlady Lynda Hall was leaving her husband, Derek

— because of a ghost which pulls pints. Lynda said that the ghost also flushes toilets, jams doors and wanders around the bedrooms, and every morning it leaves a glass upside down on the bar of their pub, the Ship Inn at Swinton, near Mexborough.

The ghost is thought to be that of a former landlord who died behind the bar some years ago and Lynda wanted Derek to call a clergyman to exorcize it. She said, 'It's becoming more and more unnerving and it has scared me to death. I'm leaving and I'm not coming back until Derek has got rid of it.'

Over 150 years ago, a crowd of townsfolk stood around the gallows which had been erected in the yard of the Feathers. They had come from the surrounding districts to witness the demise of a highwayman, convicted not for highway robbery, but for the particularly nasty murder of a serving wench from the old inn. Since that day, the old pub at Pocklington, about sixteen miles from York, has been haunted by a ghost which the locals are convinced is that of the highwayman.

Room number 7 has an uncanny atmosphere about it and many residents have refused to sleep there after the first night. Sounds of heavy breathing are heard, as if someone is trying to pull a heavy object along the corridor. The atmosphere in the room becomes so frightening, that although nothing is seen, the unfortunate occupant is unable, through fear, to get out of bed to investigate.

Out on the Yorkshire Moors, about ten miles north of Pickering one will find a signpost showing the way to Saltergate. At the bottom of the Devil's Elbow stands the only building for miles, the Saltergate Inn, built around 1760 and known until recent years as the Waggon and Horses. The inn, well known for its cuisine as well as its associations with the old salt smugglers, is also famed for its ghostly legend, thanks to Brenda English's lively book set in Saltergate in the eighteenth century, *Crying in the Wilderness*.

No apparition has been seen at the inn, but there can often be heard, outside on the silent moors, the sound of a woman crying. When the inn was built, the very first landlord lit a peat fire, which right up to the present day has not been allowed to go out, for it is said that should this be allowed to happen, great misfortune would fall on the inn and its inhabitants. Local legend says that the fire keeps an evil spirit imprisoned beneath the hearth, the spirit of a witch who was buried on the spot where the inn now stands and whose malignant ghost is kept at bay by the smouldering peat.

Near the old harbour at Scarborough, tucked away up a narrow alleyway, stands a rather unique museum. This building was, until earlier this century, an inn, the Three Mariners. This fascinating old inn, built in 1300, is riddled with bolt-holes, secret passages and concealed cupboards, which in the old days were used by smugglers and sailors wishing to avoid the authorities or the press gangs. Tradition has it that a tunnel runs from the old harbour to the inn, which was used to smuggle the American John Paul Jones to safety after his ship, *Le Bonhomme Richard* was sunk by a superior British squadron off Flamborough Head.

However, of more interest to the ghost hunter, is the room which is reputed to be haunted by the ghost of a headless woman, who is said to have appeared on several occasions to warn the local fishermen not to put to sea. One story tells of two fishermen who, setting off early to a day's work, saw the headless spectre as they approached the Three Mariners in the early morning mist. Seeing her, one of the fishermen refused to go any further and returned home for the rest of the day. His partner laughed and poured scorn on the unfortunate man, saying that he was more afraid of what his wife would say if he returned home empty-handed than he was of the headless ghost. He continued on his way down to the quay and took his boat out to sea, only to be drowned later in the day, when a sudden squall caught his boat and turned it over off Yons Nab.

I understand that when the building was still in use as an inn, many people reported seeing the headless ghost in the haunted room. One woman complained that an unseen hand had snatched the clothes from her bed in the early hours of the morning. No one knows who the headless woman is and today no one will admit to having seen her recently. However the fishermen still look for her as they make their way down to the quay for a day's fishing.

At Sutton near Cleckheaton, there is an old pub said to be haunted by a phantom, known locally as the 'dripping innkeeper'. It appears that many years ago when the old innkeeper lay dying, he called for his only son and requested that after his death his body should be placed in a watertight coffin filled with ale. The son promised he would carry out his father's wish and when at last the old man died, he spoke of it to all who came to pay their last respects.

Now, being Yorkshire men, the idea of all that good ale being wasted on a corpse instead of going down the throats of the mourners, was more than they could cope with and they threatened to boycott not only the funeral, but the inn. The son, being the heir to the business, was also a practical man and he couldn't help but feel he would soon go bankrupt if he carried out his father's wish, so he compromised and filled the coffin with water.

Since that day, it is said the pub has been haunted by the

ghost of the old innkeeper who, even today, materializes dripping wet and seeking to wreak vengeance on all those who deprived him of his last drink of ale.

The Cock and Bottle Inn at York stands on the site of a much older Plumbers Arms, demolished some time ago. Who built the older pub isn't really known, but it is known to have stood in the grounds of a large house in Bishophill.

History tells us that the infamous George Villiers, second Duke of Buckingham, stayed here at some time and used it as a centre for alchemy in his efforts to turn base metals into gold. The odds are that he also did a bit of black magic on the side, for he certainly appears to have left some evil influences behind him.

Despite being a favourite at the Court of Charles II, Villiers died a disgraced pauper. He spent his last years in York but it was actually at Kirkby Moorside that he died, his body being taken to Westminster for burial in a pauper's grave, although his shade has returned to the York that he loved.

Some very frightening events take place at the Cock and Bottle, besides the more mundane opening and closing of doors, bangs, thumps, footsteps and the inevitable cold draughts. A man wearing a wide-brimmed hat has been seen quite often who suddenly evaporates and anyone wearing a crucifix on the premises is quite likely to have it roughly snatched from them by unseen hands. I was told that one man was seized by an invisible force in an upstairs passage and pinned to the spot for several minutes, during which time he saw the apparition of a milkmaid, carrying a yoke and buckets. Some time in 1972 a skeleton was found nearby on the site of the Duke of Buckingham's library, which might possibly have some connection with the hauntings.

Behind Selby Abbey stands one of the oldest pubs in the town, the Crown Hotel, where several unusual occurrences have taken place in the last few years.

The present licensees, Ronnie and Joyce Whitaker, told me that not long after they moved in, in January 1977, they were disturbed by heavy footsteps several times during the night. At first they thought they were coming from the premises next door, until they discovered they were empty. Nothing much was thought about it until lunchtime on Christmas Day, 1978, when both Ronnie and his wife, and a number of customers, saw a picture on the wall behind the bar detach itself and fly across the bar to smash on the floor. This was a picture of the pub, which had been taken around the turn of the century.

A barman was frightened one night by a grey figure of a woman, which materialized at one corner of the bar and just as suddenly evaporated. Ronnie explained that earlier this century a landlord murdered his wife in the bar, after a heavy drinking session one Christmas, and it is thought to be her ghost which now haunts this old riverside pub.

The Fleece Inn at Elland, has a permanent reminder of a foul deed perpetrated there many years ago. An old beggar, known as 'Leathery Coit' because of his tanned, leathery skin caused through spending a lifetime on the moors, was brutally murdered in one of the upstairs rooms and his body dragged down a flight of wooden stairs, leaving a trail of blood which no amount of scrubbing could remove. Old 'Leathery Coit's' ghost has been seen in the pub and in nearby Dog Lane.

For a number of years, there were reports of a ghost, dressed like a Victorian gentleman, haunting the cellars of the old Golden Lion that used to stand in North Street, Leeds. The ghost of an old lady, her hair done in ringlets was also seen in one of the bedrooms.

It is believed the two spectres were a husband and wife who lived on the premises in the early part of the century and who loved the old place so much they were loth to leave it, even in death. The pub has now been pulled down and I have been unable to locate its actual site, but I wouldn't mind betting that before long, someone in the glass and concrete jungle now built over the area, will report seeing a lady whose hair is done in ringlets and a gentleman dressed in Victorian clothes.

Howley Hall Golf Club, near Batley, was once the farm-house belonging to Howley Hall, the sixteenth-century home of Sir John Savile, first mayor of Leeds. In 1643, the Duke of Newcastle demanded the house be handed over to the King, a demand which was scorned by Sir John and which caused the deaths of several stout defenders, when it was blasted to smithereens by cannon fire. What was left of the estates was let out to various families including the well-known Villiers. One of them, Lady Anne Villiers, was said to have accidentally drowned whilst bathing in a nearby spring.

One afternoon a few years ago, the figure of a woman wearing a long dress, with a dark top and veil over her head and shoulders, was seen near the ruins before suddenly fading from sight. Two men and a woman were seen one evening by a man walking his dog. These figures, dressed in seventeenth-century clothes, vanished when he approached them. Whether these are the ghosts of members of the Villiers family, or whether they are the ghosts of the defenders of Howley Hall is not certain, but I think the latter would be most likely.

The Royal Hotel at Armley, Leeds, has a frightening ghost of a grey lady, who appears from time to time. One night in

1972, a young barman got the fright of his life when he went into the cellars to turn off the beer pumps and saw the dim figure of a woman slowly taking shape before his astonished eyes and staring fixedly at him for several seconds.

Stories have been told of this ghost for many years, but it was only recently that it was discovered that in 1858 the then landlord of the Royal Hotel had shot his mistress on the premises.

The Weaver's Restaurant, at Haworth, formerly The Toby Jug, boasts the one ghost I would most like to meet, that of the novelist, Emily Brontë, who was brought up at the parsonage, less than a hundred yards away. Emily's ghost is said to appear each year, on the anniversary of her death, December 19th. She was first reported as being seen in 1966, when the owner saw a small figure in a crinoline, carrying a wicker basket and smiling and giggling, cross the room to where the staircase used to be and begin to climb up to the bedroom above. He recognized her as Emily from her portrait which was painted by her brother Branwell and which still hangs in the parsonage museum.

However Colin and Jane Rushworth, the present owners, told me that, although they stayed up to see her on December 19th, 1978, she failed to materialize.

Also at Haworth, the Sun Inn was said to be haunted for many years. The interior was altered somewhat during the early 1970s and when it was re-opened, the new landlord was told of the ghost by the locals. He was very sceptical, but just to be on the safe side, he had a good luck charm, in the shape of a gargoyle, placed over the door, but refuses to say whether this has been successful or not!

Just north of Easingwold stands a lovely old private house, known as the White House. During the seventeenth century, it was a coaching inn, run·by a man called Ralph Reynard. The building has obviously changed quite a bit since those days, but it only needs a little imagination to visualize how it must have looked back in the 1620s when the events took place which gave rise to its ghost.

Ralph Reynard courted a flighty, buxom, dark-haired servant girl from Thornton Bridge. Seemingly all went well, until one day the two lovers quarrelled and the girl broke off their relationship. In due course she met and married a farmer called Fletcher, of Moor House. She had no real love for him and, as time went by, the young Mrs Fletcher began to realize her mistake in marrying him and wished instead that she had continued her romance with Ralph.

One day, she and Ralph met quite by accident and in the course of time they became reconciled, but of course it was too late and Reynard was left to brood alone at the inn. As time went by, the villagers began to notice that Mrs Fletcher's horse was often to be seen tethered outside the inn, and it wasn't long before the inevitable happened and Fletcher found out about the affair between his wife and Reynard.

Determined to put a stop to it once and for all, Fletcher made for the White House Inn, but on reaching Dauney Bridge, was set upon by Reynard and his ostler, Mark Duncan. He was knocked off his horse into the stream and his two assailants jumped in after him, holding his head under the water until he drowned. The two men and Mrs Fletcher, who had remained hidden during the killing, then made their way back to Easingwold with the body of the unfortunate Fletcher wrapped in sacking, and there, under cover of darkness, buried him in the garden of the inn.

Several times after this, Reynard was confronted by the ghost of Fletcher, who would point an accusing finger at him and intone in a deep voice, 'Oh Ralph, oh Ralph,

The Westbourne Road studios of BBC Radio Sheffield, where amongst the non-stop working atmosphere of today, something or somebody lingers.

Marilyn and Peter Auty, who for the past eight years have shared their delightful cottage with an unidentified ghost.

(left): The haunted landing at Greenfield Lodge where a woman has been seen going up the stairs on several occasions. This old house is thought to be haunted by the ghost of Elizabeth Emmett.

(below): East Riddlesdon Hall. It was here that Mr M. Atkins encountered the ghost of the unidentified woman in blue.

Skulls in the gateway to the churchyard at Hickleton. Thought to be associated with the ghost of a highwayman who haunts the area and was seen by the author.

Should you see the ghost of Lady Anne Clifford riding up Skipton main street, you can expect to hear quite soon of the death of the Lord of the Honour.

26 Bowling Green, Stainland. It was in this house that Albert Paradise saw the ghost of the violinist on New Year's Eve 1956. The houses have now been demolished. Mr Paradise can be seen chatting at the front gate.

(left): Mr Albert Paradise, an authority on the history of Stainland, who was confronted by a phantom violinist on New Year's Eve 1956.

(below): The 'Olde Silent Inn', Stanbury. Famous for its association with Bonnie Prince Charlie and its soothing ghost.

The 'Cock and Bottle Inn', York. Associated with the infamous George Villiers, who has left an evil influence on the place.

The 'Sun Inn', Haworth. The landlord placed a gargoyle over the entrance when he heard that the inn was haunted, but refuses to say whether or not it worked.

The 'Weavers Restaurant', Haworth. Thought to be haunted by the ghost of the novelist Emily Bronte.

Bolton Priory. Here the figure of a monk is often seen in the ruined choir, usually in the month of July.

The rectory, Bolton Priory. Here in 1912, the Marquis of Hartington saw the ghost of an old man with a heavily wrinkled face. King George V showed a lot of interest in this ghost.

Holy Trinity Church, York. Haunted by the ghost of its last Abbess, a mother and child and a male wearing a surplice.

York Minster. Home of many ghosts, the most famous being Dean Gale.

The Merrion Centre, Leeds. Built on the site of the Camp Hill area of the town, a derelict maze of mid-Victorian back-to-back terraces. Here a ghost of an old man was seen, tending roses amidst the ruins, in mid-November, 1945.

(left): The rocking chair is the favourite haunt of the comfort-seeking spectre. This one has been seen rocking of its own accord.

(below): The Theatre Royal, York. Built on the site of the old St Leonards Hospital founded by King Stephen in the 12th Century. Haunted by the ghost of a nun and an actor who died in a duelling accident.

The famous City of Varieties Theatre, Leeds. A theatre of mystery which contains at least two ghosts.

repent. Vengeance is at hand!' After meeting the ghost again at Topcliffe Fair, Reynard was terrified for his life and galloped home. As he went, the spectre glided ahead of him, trailing a sack behind it, until on reaching the inn the apparition walked through the hedge and with a sigh dissolved into the ground where the body was buried.

Arriving at the inn, Reynard confessed all to his sister who, horrified at what her brother had told her, had no hesitation in notifying the local magistrate, who lived at nearby Raskelf Park.

On July 28th, 1623, Mrs Fletcher, Ralph Reynard and Mark Duncan were hanged at York and their bodies were suspended from the gibbet at Gallows Hill. The ghost of Fletcher, however, remained on at the White House Inn for many years afterwards. For a good number of years coach horses would show fear on approaching the place and today, as a private dwelling, 'White Walls' is still said to be influenced by the events which took place here all those years ago, although the ghost of Fletcher has not been seen for a good number of years.

The Wyke Non-Political Club at Bradford is haunted by a ghost known to all as 'Fred', who first made his presence known in 1972. Shortly before midnight a member of the staff decided to visit the ladies' room before leaving for home. As she opened the door she saw, standing a few feet from her, a grey-haired man in a dark suit, with staring eyes and bedraggled clothing, which gave him a sinister appearance. Turning to run from the room, the frightened woman felt a cold hand under hers on the door knob, a cold hand with four fingers, but no thumb; The poor women fainted through sheer terror.

Other strange things have happened here. One morning a table with four chairs around it, was found on the stage. No member of staff had put them there. Four wet rings were found on the table, but there were no glasses to be found nearby. A cleaner, having finished cleaning the dressing rooms, was returning to the main hall of the club, when she almost ran into the figure of a man sitting on some steps, with his head in his hands. The lights in the building have turned off and on by themselves and there is often an atmosphere and a feeling of being watched by unseen eyes.

Whose ghost is this? Well, it appears that the club was built on the site of a dyehouse and mill dam. Years ago a millwright, who had lost the thumb off one hand, was accidentally drowned in the dam. Why he is determined to scare the daylights out of the staff is a mystery, although some people think he might be resentful of the changes that have taken place since the dyehouse was pulled down.

Not far from Westgate, Wakefield, is the Grove Inn, where quite a number of extraordinary occurrences have taken place, as a result of a ghost taking up residence there in the latter part of the 1950s. There are also suggestions of poltergeist activities, for heavy furniture has been moved, mirrors smashed and things have been thrown about as if by a naughty child.

One lady complained of waking in terror and feeling as if she were being smothered by an invisible being. On another occasion three boys sleeping in the same room complained of a similar feeling. No one knows who or what this ghost is, or why he should suddenly become attached to the pub, but whenever anything untoward happens, 'Fred', as he is called, is sure to be blamed.

Just outside Sheffield at Kiverton Park, stands the Saxon Hotel, built in the early 1960s and haunted by an unusual whistling ghost. Successive landlords have heard enough to convince them that the place is haunted.

The ghost is thought to be that of a monk who was murdered hereabouts many years ago, and it is believed he was connected with the chantry which at one time stood on the site of the hotel. 'He' is nearly always experienced in the cellars, when his presence is made known by a distinctive whistle, as if he is trying to attract attention. Sometimes his presence is so overpowering that anyone in the cellar quickly leaves it, to seek reassurance in the comfort of the bar. Although 'The Whistler', as the ghost has become known locally, has never invaded the privacy of the landlord's quarters, he can often be heard padding down the cellar steps, seemingly as if wearing carpet slippers.

The Blue Ball Inn, at Soyland, is an isolated eighteenth-century inn with nineteenth-century additions, and stands on the ancient Blackstone Edge pack horse road, near Ripponden. Here in 1766, James Procter wove shalloons, worsted cloth used chiefly for coat linings. Later the inn became known as 'Rudman's Place', a popular eating house. Fugitives from Halifax with Royalist troops in hot pursuit fled this way in 1643, as did Daniel Defoe in the 1700s.

The Blue Ball is said to be haunted by the ghost of a serving wench, who worked here for a notorious landlord known as 'Iron Will', some time in the eighteenth century. 'Iron Will' was a renowned lecher and he is said to have raped the girl and then drowned her on the moors. Faith, as she was called, can be heard on quiet nights during the winter, running across the floor of what some people say was 'Iron Will's' bedroom, presumably to escape from his amorous advances.

The Ribblesdale Arms at Gisburn, built in 1635 by Thomas Lister, boasts a bed with foot carvings which resemble small children dressed in shrouds and the ghost of a young girl. Needless to say, both can be found in room number thirteen.

Legend tells us that one Lord Ribblesdale, a rake and a waster, seduced a young local girl in this bedroom, who became pregnant as a result. The theory now is that although Lord Ribblesdale is long dead, and buried in a silver coffin, the ghost of the girl returns seeking to avenge herself. Although the ghost has not been seen in recent years, the proprietors take no chances and don't let the room, unless pressed to do so. Even then they have taken the precaution of fitting a bell behind the bed, so that in the event of any ghost hunter, or innocent guest for that matter, finding themselves in difficulty, they can ring for assistance.

Finally, for the last ghost in this chapter, we visit the Angel Inn at old Catterick village, which was, in its time, the largest coaching house in the area. Despite its size, it only catered for two stagecoaches and its long row of stables was used by breeders and race-goers. The Angel also had at one time a cockpit and there are tales told of huge wagers being laid on rowdy nights following a day's racing.

The Angel was haunted by the ghost of a nun, thought by many to be connected with the name of the inn. According to local legend, the nun was imprisoned below the church for being over-familiar with a priest from St Martin's Church, nearby. I am told there used to be a tunnel connecting the church with the inn; and it was along this tunnel that the ghost of the nun was said to walk.

The haunted inns of Yorkshire would fill several volumes, but sadly there is no further room in this book for more than just a small selection. However, should the reader happen to visit any of them during a leisurely summer's drive, take a good look at the person sitting quietly and alone at the next table . . . After all, it might only be me, but then, on the other hand . . . !

CHAPTER 6

Mary Queen of Scots and Turret House

There are many alleged hauntings by the unhappy Royal prisoner, Mary Queen of Scots. Like Elizabeth I, her ghost pops up wherever she is supposed to have stayed prior to her execution. Few hauntings can be authenticated but others, like the ghost that haunts the Turret House, attached to the old manor castle at Sheffield, can be authenticated by historical fact and eyewitness account.

By the fifteenth century, the Earls of Shrewsbury had acquired the castle and when the third Earl died in 1473, at the age of twenty-six, he left a son, George, who became the fourth Earl at the tender age of five. George married the daughter of his guardian, Lord Hastings, and took up residence at the castle, where he lived throughout the reign of Henry VII.

He was a man who liked his comforts and he felt the great castle was too spartan by far. We know the young Tudors liked comfortable living and George was no exception, preferring glass in his windows, large comfortable beds and chairs which conformed to the contours of the human anatomy. He therefore built himself a more comfortable residence in the castle park, which subsequently became known as Manor Lodge.

Manor Lodge was furnished magnificently throughout. Two hundred and forty 'Crowns of the sun' were spent on wall hangings alone. The forlorn remains which now stand in Manor Lane bear little comparison to the original, but the armorial overmantle and plaster ceilings of the Turret House give some indication of the ornamentation the house contained.

The Turret House was built as a porter's lodge by Earl Gilbert, although many people believe that it was built especially to house the unhappy prisoner Mary Queen of Scots. There is evidence to show that Mary was indeed held captive here. She was handed over to Earl George Talbot, grandson of the fourth Earl of Shrewsbury, at Tutbury in 1569 and was incarcerated in Sheffield Castle itself on November 28th, 1570. She had brought numerous retainers with her, though their number was cut down to thirty on the orders of Queen Elizabeth.

Now the castle became a prison, not only for the poor Scottish Queen, but also for the young Earl and his wife, Bess of Hardwick, whom he had married in 1568, because the slightest relaxation of vigilance set the Royal prisoner plotting her escape. As a result of this she was eventually moved into the Turret House.

History records she spent nearly fourteen years a prisoner of the Earl and by 1584 he had had enough and petitioned Queen Elizabeth to release him from this intolerable duty. Elizabeth agreed and no doubt with great relief, Earl George transferred Mary into the custody of Sir John Somers and Sir Ralph Sadler.

Mrs Ida Elliott, of Sheffield, spent quite some time at Turret House with her late husband's relatives who during the 1930s were retainers of the late Duke of Northumberland, having spent many years in service to the Estate. She told me: 'As I remember it, the place was very gruesome and my in-laws used to tell me some hair-raising stories of unaccountable happenings. None of them would stay in the place alone, day or night.'

Mrs Elliott went on to say that on the Sunday following the Coronation of King George VI, she was at Turret House, having been invited with her husband to have tea with his mother and an old aunt who lived with her. During conversation the aunt said, quite casually, that she had seen the ghost of Mary Queen of Scots on the night of the Coronation. No one but Mrs Elliott appeared the least bit surprised, but she sensed they felt a little uneasy when she pressed the old lady to tell her more about it. However, persistence won the day and she was told that the aunt had been sitting up in bed drinking her cocoa when the apparition appeared, dressed in a long black dress and looking very beautiful, and glided across the room, evaporating into the opposite wall. Mrs Elliott asked her mother-in-law, who shared the room, whether she too had seen the ghost, but although she did not deny it she refused to discuss it further.

'As time went by and I got to know the family more, I asked if I could stay the night with them,' said Mrs Elliott, 'but I was always given a flat "no". When I asked them why not, the only reply I would get, was that it was an evil house with very strange happenings and friends who had stayed there in the past had run out of the house in the early morning hours, refusing to go back, even in daylight.' Some years later, Mrs Elliott met one of these people and she was told that although they had not actually seen anything, each time they were dropping off to sleep, they had the sensation that someone was trying to smother them and they had to fight off an unseen intruder.

During the 1930s, Turret House was, unlike today, set more or less in open country and to reach it one had to walk along a long drive. Apart from one or two farms and their outbuildings, it was surrounded by fields. Mrs Elliott said, 'My mother-in-law used to tell me that at twilight, one could often glance at the window and see someone, dressed in what appeared to be a cape and a cowl, peering through at them. However, on going out to investigate, no person could be found. They soon learned to draw the curtains before lighting the oil lamps.'

At that time there used to be a stone coffin just outside the house, which was said to have been made for the Earl of Shrewsbury, who, it has been suggested, was the lover of the Scottish Queen during her period of imprisonment there. On certain days, the family dog would never go anywhere near the coffin, and if for any reason he was shut outside alone, he would howl and frantically scratch at the door, only to cower shivering with fright after being allowed into the house.

The house itself contained only six rooms. The two on the ground floor, partly oak-panelled with thick walls and iron-studded doors, had been the guard rooms during Mary's time, but were converted in later years into a kitchen and lounge. A stone, spiral staircase led to two rooms on the first floor. These were used by the family as bedrooms. Two further rooms, unoccupied, made up the second floor. These two rooms were said to have been the rooms where the Scottish Queen was held. The staircase continued up into the turret and led on to a flat roof, which was the only place where poor Mary could exercise in the open air. Mrs Elliott said, 'As I remember it, her sitting room was quite ornate with a magnificent fireplace. On the chimney breast was depicted her own coat of arms. The ceiling was of ornate plaster with various symbols and Latin phrases incorporated in it. The windows were diamond leaded and heavily barred, but in each diamond-shaped glass there was a red Tudor rose. These windows made the room very dark and dismal and one could see little through them.'

In one of these rooms was a very old incense burner, which had probably been in use since long before Mary's time to keep away evil spirits. Made from stone, it was about two feet tall and cut in the shape of an imp. Smoke from the incense came out of gaping sockets where the eyes and mouth should have been. On a number of occasions everyone in the house was awakened by unaccountable noises coming from the rooms on the top floor. Fearing intruders, the men of the house hurriedly dressed and went to investigate, only to find nothing amiss.

One night, having been disturbed they went and checked and found as before that nothing was wrong, so they went back to bed. After a while the noises started up again, but louder and more persistent. Mrs Elliott continued: 'Up they went again. There was still no one there, but they were convinced that the old incense burner had been moved to a different part of the room.'

However, after a lengthy discussion they decided that perhaps they had imagined it after all, and to make absolutely sure they drew a chalk circle around it on the stone floor before once more going back to their warm beds. 'They were disturbed throughout the night,' said Mrs Elliott, 'but they decided to ignore it until the next morning, when on investigation they found the incense burner, which was too heavy for them to move, was completely outside the chalk circle.'

Turret House still stands, but it is now derelict and uninhabited, except by rats and mice. The Duke of Norfolk bequeathed it to the Sheffield Corporation, but the cost of restoration and maintenance was too much for them to be able to do anything with it. The farms and fields which once surrounded it are now gone and modern housing estates have replaced them. The twentieth century has at last caught up with it.

Does the sad Scottish Queen still wander about those upper floor rooms seeking solace, or plotting escape? Or has she, too, succumbed to a modern way of life which seems to have no place in it for antiquity?

CHAPTER 7

Ghostly Monks and Phantom Nuns

Phantom monks are ten-a-penny in the British Isles. Most ruined abbeys and monasteries claim one and several have been recorded on film. In the 'red rose' county, perhaps the best known and probably the best documented of all these phantom monks is the ghost of the Black Canon who haunts Bolton Priory in Wharfedale.

Each year many thousands of holiday makers visit this beautiful ruin which stands alongside the Wharfe, in what is considered to be one of the most scenic parts of the county. The whole area is a delight to the eye and one can never leave without thinking how peaceful the Priory must have been in days gone by. But, visit the site as I have done after dark, when the moon casts shadows beneath archways and doorways and even the most hardened and unimaginative will feel a cold shiver run down their spine, for on these occasions it doesn't need much encouragement for the imagination to run riot.

The Augustinian Canons made a start on their priory at Embsay, a few miles away, on land bequeathed to them by Cecilly de Romille in about 1120. Round about 1160, the de Romille family provided new lands beside the River Wharfe and the canons decided that this was a far better site for their church. By moving there they provided work for many local craftsmen on and off for the next three or four hundred years.

Following the Battle of Bannockburn, the priory was plundered by the Scots and it was not until about 1330 that life was resumed here again and a new band of men-at-arms was trained to defend the priory and surrounding lands against all enemies. During the Dissolution of the Monasteries, the Brothers were sent packing, but the Prior managed to stay on and complete his work alone. Perhaps this is why a small part of the building was allowed to remain intact and became the parish church.

Among the many reports from people who have claimed to have seen a ghost at the priory, particularly in the years before the First World War, the eyewitness account of the late Marquis of Hartington remains the most detailed.

In 1912, the Marquis, who was only a small boy at the time, was on holiday from his school at Eton and, with others, was a guest at the Rectory during the grouse season. The Rectory is believed to stand on the site of the old priory guest house. One night on going to his bedroom, the Marquis was surprised to see a figure standing at the bedroom door. It was a man in his late sixties, dressed in nondescript clothing with a heavily lined and wrinkled face which seemed unusually round and which might have been the face of a woman, had it not been for several days' growth of grey stubble on the chin.

The Marquis was at the top of the staircase, looking towards his room at the end of the passage. He ran downstairs for another light, but by the time he had got back to the passage again, the figure had vanished. King George V showed much interest in this ghost and although he did not see it himself he heard, with the Duke of Devonshire and Lord Desborough, the Marquis of Hartington's account of what he saw.

In 1911, one Reverend MacNabb, Rector of Bolton, was standing looking out of the windows in the Rectory, when he felt compelled to turn around. On doing so, he saw the apparition watching him from the doorway. It was seen again in 1920 by Lord Cavendish and more recently in 1965, when a man entering the gatehouse saw a figure, dressed in a black cassock with a white overlay of what looked like wool, black cloak and flat black hat, walking towards him. The figure has also been seen in the ruined choir, in the priory grounds and in the precincts of the church and the sound of sandaled feet is often heard in the Rectory.

Most of the more recent sightings have been in broad daylight, usually in the month of July, but although I went over every inch of the site in July 1979 and again in 1980, I'm afraid I must report being disappointed.

Fountains Abbey, near Harrogate, is also only a ruin now, albeit one of the most magnificent ruins to be found in Yorkshire. It was once the richest Cistercian Abbey in the whole of England. There is no authentic record of any apparition being seen on the site, but the sound of monks chanting an old psalm has been heard quite often, on still, quiet evenings.

The ghost of the Abbess Hilda is said to haunt the remains of her old abbey at Whitby, a majestic ruin above the sea. In summer, if one stands in Whitby churchyard, one can see the north side of the abbey, just past the north end of the church. Here, if one is lucky, one might just catch a glimpse of the Abbess, dressed in a shroud and standing in one of the highest windows.

The abbey site also gives rise to a nice little legend: Many years ago, a herdsman lay in the straw of the abbey stables feeling rather depressed. He could hear the layworkers singing and was sad because he could not join in their nightly revelries. Suddenly the stable glowed with an eerie light, which became brighter as a shining figure appeared before him and commanded him to stand up and 'sing of the beginning of created things'. The frightened herdsman ran to the abbey to report what he had seen to the Abbess. She told him the story of Genesis which he later recited in plainsong. So affected was the young herdsman by his experience, that he later became a monk. His name was Caedmon, the first English Christian poet.

Today, the sounds of a choir echo faintly in the ruins of Whitby Abbey at the hour of dawn on Christmas Day, singing the songs of Caedmon, the father of English song.

Kirkstall Abbey, near Leeds, is a fine example of Norman architecture and even though in ruins the layout of the monastic buildings are quite clearly defined.

The abbey was built in 1152 for Cistercian monks from Fountains Abbey. The church and accommodation was completed in 1182 and little is known of its history for the next four centuries. It was surrendered to the Crown in 1540 and was allowed to fall into decay until being bought by Colonel North and presented to the City of Leeds for restoration, back in the last century.

The former gate-house, which now houses the Abbey museum, is said to be haunted by the ghost of an old Abbot. One lady who worked there for a number of years, has told of strange noises which can be heard late at night, and she claims to have seen a ghost in 1935, pacing the building.

All roads through Selby lead to the Abbey, one of the finest in the country. It was built originally as a monastery by Hugh de Lacy and its origins are said to have been politically motivated. Work began in 1097 but was not finished until 1340.

In 1936, a curate was alone in the Abbey after evensong and as he cleared away vestments in the sacristy, he heard voices, followed by the sound of groaning. The young man went into the main body of the church to see if someone had been taken ill and was in need of assistance. Not a soul remained in the building, although the groaning continued. The frightened curate ran to tell the Canon of his experience and on being asked whether he should not have looked more closely into the matter, apparently replied, 'No, sir, I ran like the Devil!' Other people have had uncanny experiences here, but no explanation can be given as to the cause of these rather unnerving occurrences.

York Minster is said to have several ghosts, but the most famous is that of Dean Gale who died in the Minster in 1702 and who is buried there in a lead coffin.

Shortly after the Dean had been buried, a preacher was taking evening service. He finished reading the sermon and, as he stepped from the pulpit, he saw the old Dean sitting in his usual place. The Dean's son on hearing of the apparition would not accept the story, which had by this time caused enough of a stir to interest Samuel Pepys. Over the years this ghost has been seen sitting silently in the pew which was always used by Dean Gale.

Of course the roads of Yorkshire abound with other spectres, besides those of highwaymen. For instance, the A164 near Driffield has been the haunt of Elfrida, the headless nun, for centuries. She was said to be a beautiful young novice who fell foul of the jealous Abbess and fled the abbey with a young local blade, with whom she had fallen in love. She was said to have become pregnant and her lover, on learning this, suddenly lost his ardour and threw her out. She returned to the Abbey where, despite her remorse and pleas for forgiveness, she was sentenced to death and beheaded.

Her ghost is seen drifting through the fields near the village of Watton and if the hardy dare approach her she will turn towards them, to reveal that the inside of her flowing head-dress is empty.

Holy Trinity Church in Micklegate, York, was part of a

Benedictine Priory attached to the Abbey of Marmontier in France and is said to be haunted by the ghost of its last Abbess, a woman and a child and some say, a male figure wearing a surplice.

History records how the Abbess came to haunt the church. She defied the soldiers sent by Henry VIII to carry out his policy of dissolution, by saying they would only enter the convent over her dead body. The soldiers attacked her and as she lay dying, she promised that she would haunt the place until another sacred building rose on the spot, a promise she kept until the convent was demolished completely, when she then moved into the church. She is often seen on Trinity Sunday and often in the company of a woman and child.

There was great excitement one hot August Sunday morning in the mid-nineteenth century when a worshipper saw three figures, two women and a child, move across the east window. The two women were seen quite clearly against the window itself. One was tall and graceful and the other of average size and build, who appeared to be caressing the child as if to soothe it. No one knows who these ghosts are, although the tall graceful figure may be that of the Abbess, and the others the wife and child of a man who was buried near the organ window. Not long after his death his only child died of the plague and was buried in a great plague pit outside the walls of the city, while his wife, who also died shortly afterwards of the plague, was buried with him in his grave near the organ window. It is said that the spirit of the mother would not rest without the child and that the spirit of the Abbess brings the child from the grave outside the city to the grave of her father and mother, in Holy Trinity Church.

In 1876, a worshipper recorded having seen a bright light formed like a female, robed and hooded, glide rapidly from north to south at some distance outside the window. The figure returned some time later accompanied by the figure of the child. The child was not seen again, but the woman returned and hurriedly completed the last trip across the window.

Although these figures have not been seen for many years, the unknown figure of a man in a surplice has been seen quite recently.

Of course, not all spectral clerics are to be met in abbeys and churches, many can be found in the old halls of Yorkshire, which, like the big houses of Lancashire and Cheshire, had their connections with the church and were riddled with bolt-holes and priests' hides.

Gawthorpe Hall, Bingley (not to be confused with Gawthorpe Hall at Burnley), is haunted by the ghost of a nun who is said to have been killed by her lover. She has been seen, dressed in black cloak and hood, walking along the driveway. Likewise Ripley Castle is haunted by a mysterious, yet well-mannered nun who knocks on bedroom doors during the night. Why well-mannered? Well, unless the bleary-eyed occupant says, 'Come in,' she will not enter the room.

A monk, described as a kindly old man 'with a funny haircut', is said to haunt the upper rooms of a sixteenth-century house in Beverley and the figure of a monk has been seen at Pickering Castle as recently as 1970. The ghost was first seen in 1951, by an attendant as he sat in his room by the drawbridge of the thirteenth-century castle, one wet and miserable evening. The figure was tall and dressed in a long grey robe and his hood was pulled up over his head, making it impossible to see his face. He held his arms out as if carrying something and moved swiftly across the lawn from the direction of the keep, only to disappear on the site of the old castle ovens.

The site of Donisthorpe Hall, in Leeds, was the scene of an unusual haunting in 1970, when a team of men from the Gas Board were laying a new pipe main to the synagogue which was being built on the site. While digging a trench in which to lay the pipes, the men found a number of bones, both human and animal. The old hall had been a home for aged Jews and at the side of it stood a mausoleum. When the workmen moved the laying-out slab from it, they appear to have disturbed the spirit of one of the former occupants, for very soon afterwards three workmen saw the figure of an old Rabbi, wearing a flat-topped hat and grey cloak, watching them dig the trench. The ghostly figure was seen twice, but since the completion of the synagogue has not been seen again.

While in the Leeds area, mention should be made of a school at Crossgates which is said to be haunted by a headless nun.

In the 1830s this large rambling old building was an orphanage run by nuns. One day, two small children were locked in a small room at the top of the building as punishment for some misdemeanour, when fire broke out on the floor beneath them, leaving the two children trapped.

Hearing their screams, a young nun raced upstairs to rescue them. Fighting her way through smoke and flames, she managed to reach the room. She forced open the door, and dragged the two children clear of the flames, which by now had surrounded them. Just as she pushed the children to safety, a heavy beam fell and struck the heroic nun with such force that she was decapitated.

In recent years, the room where the nun died was the school sick-bay, but it had to be sealed off after several girls reported seeing the headless nun come through the wall and others complained of shrieks and the appearance of flames licking the walls.

A more substantial ghostly cleric made himself known to Mr F. Berridge, a retired engineer, and his wife when in 1950 they bought a small thirty-acre farm above Sowerby.

According to the deeds, the house and farm buildings were erected during the seventeenth century, but in the eighteenth century the whole place was destroyed by fire. For a long time it remained a desolate ruin, until it was bought and rebuilt by a clergyman who lived in it until his death.

All this was unknown to Mr and Mrs Berridge at the time, because the deeds to the property were deposited with the bank as collateral and it was not until many years later, when they sold the farm, that they were able to see them and learn the history of the old place. Of course, in those early days they were not all that interested; they enjoyed the peaceful life of the farm and the fresh air and hard work, which ensured that they both slept soundly at night.

However, Mr Berridge says, 'On several occasions, we were both awakened from our deep slumbers by a strong smell of burning, which seemed to fill the house. Alarmed and thinking the whole place was ablaze, we would quickly investigate, but could never discover any fire.' On each occasion, after checking the house, they would go outside and check the outbuildings and, although they never found any trace of fire, they always found that one of the farm animals was in some sort of trouble. He continues: 'I recall that once it was a cow which had got its tethering chain entangled in the drinking bowl and was in danger of being strangled. Another time, it was one of the sows in difficulty over farrowing, or one of the cows having trouble in calving.' Mr Berridge is certain that had he and his wife not been roused, they would almost certainly have lost a valuable animal.

They have reached the conclusion that the spirit of the

clergyman lives on at the farm, keeping a watchful and benevolent eye on the place and warning the occupants of any imminent danger. Mr Berridge concludes: We never once saw the shade of the reverend gentleman, but we know now that he was there.'

Clementhorpe is now a populous area of York, but before it was developed it was said to be visited at night by the ghost of Archbishop Scrope, who was beheaded in 1405 following his trial at Bishopsthorpe. His execution took place in a field at Clementhorpe and it was here that his remains were said to have been interred until they were moved in time to York Minster. Travellers over the centuries have claimed to have seen a coffin, covered with a black pall and fringed with white silk, slowly floating through the air. Behind it walked the robed figure of the Archbishop, reading from an open book but with no sound coming from his moving lips.

Perhaps the most persistent story of his appearance was told by Robert Johnson, a slaughterman. Robert, accompanied by a boy, was returning one night to York, after going to a farm near Bishopsthorpe to collect some sheep. On approaching Clementhorpe, they saw, in the road ahead of them, a coffin suspended in the air, moving slowly in the same direction as themselves. It tilted occasionally, as if borne on the shoulders of men who had been thrown out of step by the roughness of the road. Behind the coffin, walking with measured tread, walked a Bishop in fine linen, bearing in his hands a large open book. On and on went the strange procession, with the steady tread usually reserved for such august occasions, while the sheep kept pace, refusing to be driven past the apparition.

Robert Johnson said in later years, that he could not have been mistaken, 'for although the night was dark, it was too light to admit of mistake'.

CHAPTER 8

Psychic Phenomena

Over the years I have met many people who are gifted with prevision or second sight; the ability to foretell future events and to discern occurrences at distant places; to perceive things not visible to ordinary sight. I suspect that all of us may have it to some degree as a latent faculty that can come to the forefront in times of crisis. Although most of the people in this chapter have never seen a ghost, in the true sense of the word, all have experienced at one time or another, some form of 'psychic vision'.

A lady wrote to me from Liversedge and told me that she had visions, particularly in times of anxiety and distress. A few years ago she was posting a letter to a sick friend who lived over ninety miles away. As she popped the letter into the post box, she said she had a vivid picture of the letter bursting into flames. Several days later, she received a letter from the Post Office apologizing for the letter being damaged after a mail bag caught fire in transit. Only her address at the top of the charred letter remained recognizable.

An eighty-six-year-old gentleman wrote to me from Horsforth and told me of two experiences he had had, which have always remained in his memory.

During the First World War, he was working in a factory in Leeds when, he says, he heard a 'ping', as if a rifle bullet had ricocheted, although he doesn't recall hearing the bang as it left the rifle. Later in the day, his younger brother came to the factory to tell him that they had just received a telegram from the War Office to say that his other brother, Hugh, was missing somewhere in Flanders. It later transpired that their brother had been killed by a sniper's bullet and his body had sunk into the stinking Flanders mud.

The second incident happened many years later when, on driving through Aberford with a friend, he had a distinct vision of his sister through the windscreen of the car. He remarked to his friend that he was sure something had happened to her and it was no surprise when he got home, to learn that his sister had collapsed and died at exactly the time he had seen the vision.

Mr Norman Lancaster, of Huddersfield, told me his late wife had been psychic and had the ability to see things which were very strange indeed.

In the spring of 1963, both he and his wife had been to a cricket match and had arranged to go on to his wife's mother's home for tea. On their way there, they passed a wood which was full of bluebells, so they stopped to pick a bunch. They then continued on their way, when suddenly Mrs Lancaster stopped dead in her tracks and threw the flowers away. He told me: 'A strange look came into her eyes and she just said two words, "Mother's dead!" ' When they finally arrived at her mother's home, a neighbour was waiting for them with the sad news that she had found Mrs Lancaster's mother dead on the floor earlier in the afternoon.

Mr Lancaster is sure his wife's spirit lives on at their home. One night he was sitting alone watching television, when he distinctly heard his wife's voice saying, 'Are you there, Norman?' He said, 'On several occasions since, I have felt a hand on my shoulder and can only think that it is my wife, God bless her.'

Miss Doreen Bennett, of Leeds, related an interesting

experience she had while visiting an old lady who lived nearby and who was practically blind. Miss Bennett told me that she noticed the old lady's eyes seemed to be looking out of the window and moving as if she was watching some activity outside. She asked if she could see something and was surprised when the old lady told her she could see a courtyard and a stagecoach. People were getting out of it, wearing Georgian-style clothes. The men wore satin breeches and jackets with lace around the wrists, the ladies wore crinolines. Nothing unusual in this, one might think. But what the old lady didn't know, was that her back garden was on the site of the courtyard of one of the last coaching inns in this part of Yorkshire.

A blind lady called at a house in Huddersfield and asked to speak to a Mrs Shackleton. She had got the wrong house, as Mrs Shackleton lived next door. However, the neighbour, realizing the blind lady's difficulty, asked her in and offered to pop next door and bring Mrs Shackleton to her.

Mrs Shackleton told me: 'I thought I was having my leg pulled, but when I went back to my neighbour's house, I was surprised to find a very small and very old lady waiting for me. She told me she had a message from someone called Mary, who was now in the next world.' Mrs Shackleton knew without doubt that the old lady was talking about her late grandmother. 'She told me many things. Things she couldn't in any way have found out beforehand,' she said.

The old lady left, declining any assistance in finding her way home. Where she came from, who she was or how she knew of Mrs Shackleton, no one dared hazard a guess. About a week later, the mysterious old lady was under discussion and Mrs Shackleton asked if any of the company present knew of her. Someone said, 'Oh yes. She used to live down Whitestone Lane. She died a few days ago!' Mrs Shackleton said that while the old lady was talking to her, she had said that she hadn't much time in which to give her the message and must have died only a day or so later.

Mr Barry Wildsmith, of Batley, was for over ten years a clairvoyant medium and during this time he experienced hundreds of instances of psychic phenomena. Although he could not relate to me for obvious reasons cases involving individuals, he was very willing to talk about experiences concerning his own immediate family.

Some years ago his two-and-a-half year-old daughter, Lynn, died following a long illness. A few months after her death, Mr Wildsmith was sitting in the kitchen when he distinctly felt someone grasp the back of his chair and shake it quite forcibly, almost enough to dislodge him on to the floor. Some minutes later, he went into the living room and saw, to his amazement, a small dark figure standing on the living-room table. His immediate reaction was to assume it was his young son, Stephen, and he called out, 'Get down off that table, before you fall off it!' But before he had finished the sentence, he realized with a shock that the figure he saw was not his son at all, but was that of his daughter. His son in fact was leaning on the same table, with his head and arms a few inches from her yet quite unaware of her presence!

Mr Wildsmith said, 'Around this time, I was again alone in the house listening to the record player and my wife, Christine, was outside in the garden. Suddenly, I lost my balance for some inexplicable reason and almost fell to the floor. On going outside I discovered that my wife too had fallen, having lost her balance at the top of the steps leading to the back door of the house.'

After the Second World War, the Camp Hill area of Leeds was nothing more than a derelict maze of back-to-back, mid-Victorian terraced houses. In 1945 many of them were pulled down and I remember as a youngster playing with my mates among the shells of these slum dwellings.

In November 1945, another group of youngsters was playing here, jumping from rafter to rafter of the upper floors, now bereft of floorboards. One of the boys, looking down through a gap where a window had been, was surprised to see, instead of the piles of rubble, bricks and half-burnt timbers, a well-kept garden about fifteen to twenty yards square, with roses in bloom and an old gentleman attending them.

As anyone who knew the Camp Hill area before and immediately after the war will tell you, the thought of flowers growing there would have been ludicrous, but at the time the fact that here was a garden full of roses in bloom in late November did not strike the boy as odd as the thought uppermost in his mind was to avoid being caught by the old man. Shouting to his mates he quickly made his way out of the house, before the old man could see him . . . Later, thinking about it, reality suddenly dawned. He searched the area, but there was no break in the heaps of waste and debris and try as he may, he could not imagine any of the obstinate scrub turning into bushes, let alone rose bushes in full bloom.

Was this a trick of the mind or a flashback into the past? The Merrion Centre now covers the area and even though I lived here in the old days I find it impossible to trace the exact location of the streets, let alone the site where a garden might have been long before the terraced houses were built in Victoria's day.

There are many stories just like these, told across the country. People claim to have predicted many things from the sinking of the *Titanic* to the murder of Earl Mountbatten. Many claim to have found lost objects and missing persons, using their psychic powers and I can well imagine the sceptics among my readers thinking to themselves, 'Ah yes. Anyone can be wise after the event.'

That these stories are difficult to prove, I am the first to admit, for until recently I too tended to look upon second sight and prevision with a rather jaundiced eye. That is, until an incident occurred while I was researching for this book, an incident which not only left me more open-minded, but stopped me in my tracks.

A remarkable lady phoned me from Bradford one evening. Verging on hysteria, she explained how during the day she had been into Bradford to do some shopping and at 5 o'clock that same afternoon had passed through a certain part of the city. Suddenly she had been overcome with a dreadful sense of fear and felt a numbing coldness surrounding her. It was obvious, even to me, that she was thoroughly distressed about the whole incident and she felt that something terrible was about to happen.

As a psychic researcher, one gets letters and telephone calls from all kinds of people, some seeking help, some seeking notoriety, some describing experiences or telling me of ghosts I had not previously come across. This lady didn't fall into any of those categories, and by her manner I was convinced she wasn't a crank either. Following our conversation, I pondered about it for a while, intending to contact her again after a couple of days to see whether anything had indeed happened.

In the event I didn't need to bother, for on the front page of my daily paper the following morning, I was shocked to discover that the so-called 'Yorkshire Ripper' had struck in Bradford overnight. A phone call confirmed that the victim had been killed within a few yards of where this lady had been standing at 5 o'clock the previous afternoon and where she had felt the overpowering feeling of coldness and fear!

If the reader finds that difficult to believe, then consider the experiences of the parents of an eleven-year-old girl living in Sheffield. A bright, pert child with dark hair and intelligent hazel eyes. Looking at her she appears very much like my own daughter did at her age, except that she is different. Uncannily different.

The girl, whom I will call Julie, has been psychic since she was eighteen months old, when, sitting on the floor one day, she suddenly looked up and said, 'Picture fall, mummy.' She crawled across to her mother just in time to avoid being hit by a large picture which came crashing down off the wall, seconds later. Coincidence? Perhaps.

Some time later, Julie was taken to the City Road Cemetery to visit her grandfather's grave. As they walked between the rows of gravestones, Julie suddenly said, 'My friend David's buried up there.' Her mother asked her to show her, so Julie took her mother's arm and led the way up a long slope and over to the other side of the graveyard, where she pointed to a worn gravestone. The legend on it read 'DAVID beloved son of Clara and Frank. Died 1903, aged 18 months.'

Julie's parents questioned her about David. How did she know about the gravestone beyond the hill? But all she would say was what she always says, 'I know,' and nothing more. Yet another coincidence?

Another time, Julie's mother went into the kitchen and found her daughter staring at a table mat with a picture of Westminster Abbey on it. The little girl, who had never been to the Abbey, was talking aloud to herself . . . 'The King won't let us ring the church bells. The King's closing all our churches. If we want to partake of the Host we have to hide the priest. The King's taken all our goblets and treasures.' . . . Her dumbfounded mother realized that Julie, only eight years old at the time, was talking about the Reformation of 1517!

Still sceptical?

CHAPTER 9

If Only It Could Talk

For a number of years, my wife and I have collected old furniture which we restore as a hobby. We are not alone in this, as the number of antique and so-called antique shops to be found in even the smallest village, bears out. On obtaining a piece of furniture, we often wonder about the original owners and speculate on the tales it could tell if it could only talk, for furniture like houses absorbs the character and, sometimes, the spirit of the owner. The rocking chair seems to be the favourite among the more comfort-seeking spectres . . .

A family living near Hull bought one such chair in an auction. On returning home, it was placed at the end of a long kitchen table, facing the door. The lady of the house, on going through the kitchen a few days later, saw to her surprise an old man with dark hair and white narrow trousers, sitting in the rocking chair and looking at her with a kind of benign expression on his face. Shocked, she asked him what he wanted, but he didn't answer and shortly afterwards disappeared.

At the Busby Stoop Inn, eight miles from Northallerton, one will discover a similar chair positioned next to the piano. It is a brave or foolish man who will dare to sit on it, as it is said to be reserved for the ghost of Tom Busby who, as we have seen in Chapter 3, was hanged in 1702 for the murder of his father-in-law, Daniel Auty. It is said that whoever sits in this particular chair will be cursed by Busby's ghost and will die within a few weeks. I am told that so far, only one man has been foolish enough to challenge the curse and he died within a fortnight.

Mr T. Dignam of Sheffield, told me of a curious incident he once experienced, which concerned an old wardrobe.

On retiring to bed one night, he was disturbed by curious rapping noises which appeared to be originating from the back of his wardrobe. He says, 'I checked the inside and the exterior of the wardrobe, finding nothing that could stimulate the rapping, neither could I attribute it to contraction of the wood, as that would create its own obvious sound.' Mr Dignam felt sure the noise was caused by someone tapping their fingers lightly on the inside of the wardrobe. He continued: 'I couldn't fathom it out and so I tapped back and, to my surprise, I received an answering tap.' He then asked a series of questions, using a simple code of two raps for 'yes' and one rap for 'no'.

'Surprisingly enough the raps answered,' he said. 'I asked if it was evil, to which it replied with two raps and I held quite a conversation using the simple code.' Eventually he got into bed, because the room had become increasingly cold during this time, but the raps continued for a further ten to fifteen minutes before they finally ceased.

Mrs Denise Branks told me of a friend who had a similar experience with a piece of furniture, but for which she has offered a possible explanation.

The gentleman in question was brought up on an old farm in Pogmoor, Barnsley. He was in bed one night when he became overcome with a feeling of not being alone, although there was enough light in the room to see that no one else was present.

On his dressing table was a low mirror, more or less standing on a level with his bed and his attention was drawn to this. He said that a face appeared in the mirror that was so clear it was as if someone was looking into it, although he was the only person in the room. The face was of a beautiful young woman, with clear skin, large eyes and long dark hair. At first he experienced a stab of fear but almost as if sensing this, the young woman smiled at him and, as she did so, an overwhelming feeling of warmth crept over him, dispelling the fear which was replaced by a feeling of peace. He said, 'I just turned over, closed my eyes and went to sleep, although I felt the face was still looking at me.'

The dressing table has long been thrown out, but Mrs Branks tells me that it had been in the family for years. The solution? Well, her friend had lost his mother when only a boy and Mrs Branks thinks it could perhaps have been she who was watching over him, although I personally have some doubts because, even if he was not able to remember his mother, he must have seen photographs of her, and, as he says, the face was so clear that 'I would recognize her at once if I was ever to meet her.'

All Brontë lovers know that when Anne Brontë spent three unhappy years at Blake Hall, Mirfield, her memory of it was such that she used the Hall as the setting for her novel *The Tenant of Wildfell Hall*.

About thirty years ago, Blake Hall was demolished, but the magnificent old staircase was saved from the hands of the demolition men by an American lady and shipped to New York State, where it was re-sited in her home. The lady now claims that she has seen the ghost of Anne, wearing a long Victorian skirt, gliding up the stairs. The ghost of a Brontë in America? Perish the thought.

Piercebridge, which stands astride the Yorkshire—Durham border on the B6275, about nine miles from Scotch Corner, boasts a seventeenth-century coaching house, The George. Hanging in the bar is an old clock which was the inspiration for the song, 'My Grandfather's Clock'.

This old timepiece was made in Darlington for two brothers and was by all accounts a superb piece of craftsmanship and a perfect timekeeper. One of the brothers died and from that day on, the clock began to go wrong. The other brother lived well into his eighties but, on the day he died, the clock stopped and all efforts to make it go since have met with failure, hence the song:

The clock stopped, never to go again,
When the old man died.

Mr J.C. Kenyon of Harrogate related a rather interesting experience his father had which again involved a piece of furniture, a chest of drawers.

Many years ago his father, John Kenyon, served as coachman at Holgate Head, Kirkby Malham. One evening on entering his room, he was surprised to see a lady in period dress in the act of opening or closing a drawer in an old-fashioned chest of drawers at the foot of his bed. On his approach the apparition disappeared. Several times he returned to his room to discover this drawer open and it was subsequently discovered that this had at some time been a 'bottom drawer', which in the tradition of the old days was reserved as a repository by a girl who was anticipating marriage. Whether in this case the lady in question ever attained the state of matrimony, neither Mr Kenyon nor his father were able to say, but it seems logical to surmise that some human tragedy is associated with her reappearance as an apparition.

The story of the ghost seen in a mirror, though otherwise invisible, is fairly widely distributed. One old Whitby story tells how, about 200 years ago, after several bad fishing seasons, a group of desperate Whitby men turned to piracy, making their unfortunate victims walk the plank. On one of the unlucky ships that was attacked by the pirates, the Captain was sailing accompanied by his wife. She was wearing a beautiful silken shawl and as she walked the plank to her death one of the pirates snatched it from her slim shoulders. He took the shawl home as a present for his wife, neglecting to tell her how it came into his possession.

On the following Sunday, as the wife was dressing for church, she tried the silken shawl over her shoulders, admiring the lovely pattern and colours as it fell in graceful folds around her. Suddenly she saw in the mirror the pale and tragic face of the drowned woman looking at her over her shoulder, her white bony hand pointing an accusing finger at the shawl. We are told that the pirate's wife went mad with terror and died shortly afterwards. No one knows what happened to the shawl; perhaps it was burned, or perhaps given to some other unsuspecting fishwife.

Although poltergeist phenomena are not, strictly speaking, paranormal and apparitions are not usually encountered in poltergeist cases, there are the odd exceptions. Whichever way one looks at it though, the activities of the poltergeist can be most distressing.

A lady from Sowerby Bridge, who wishes to remain anonymous, told me of some interesting poltergeist phenomena she encountered some years ago, which concerned household furniture.

She described how, after the children's beds had been made, the next person to go upstairs would find them all untidy again. On another occasion, while everyone was watching television, the toilet roll from the bathroom unrolled itself all the way down the stairs, while still fastened to the holder on the wall in the bathroom.

As if this was not enough, all the rods came away from the staircarpet and when they were eventually replaced, one was found to be missing. Although the whole house was searched, the stair rod could not be found. Some three or four days later, the piano in the lounge was found to have been moved by some mysterious force and was at least three or four feet away from its usual place against the wall . . . the most amazing thing of all was that the missing stair rod was discovered lying twisted behind it.

A gentleman from Sheffield experienced what he thought to be at the time, a series of incidents caused by poltergeist activity, which began about four or five years ago.

He told me: 'The first incident occurred when I was staying with my son and concerns my wrist watch which, when I go to bed, I always place under my pillow near my head.' On this particular occasion, when he woke the following morning, he could find no trace of the watch. It was not until he and his son had undertaken an intensive search that they found the watch inside the pillow slip and at the opposite side of the bed to where it had been placed the previous night.

Some time later in his own home, my correspondent was awakened one night by what appeared to be the sound of rushing wind. Being half asleep he did not bother to get up to investigate, as he knew the windows were not open. He might have dismissed the whole thing as a dream if, on getting up the following morning, he had not discovered that a small wooden reading lamp which stood near the window had been overturned and the plug had been removed from the socket!

On another occasion he found a number of articles on the passenger seat of his car. These included a perfectly good Kodak camera already loaded with unused film, two different lipsticks and a 'charity' pencil which originated in the London area. Once when he had put a clean handkerchief in his breast pocket, he found it torn to shreds when he came to use it, and on two separate occasions the lining of his jacket has also been found to be badly torn.

These events were eventually put down to the mischievous spirit of an old friend who had lived in Rustington and who had died about six or seven years before these events took place. He was well known for his leg-pulling and for playing practical jokes on his friends. He was very fond of tinkering with watches and was renowned for his clumsiness in knocking anything over within his reach. The lipsticks and the camera? . . . Well, it appears that an amorous courting couple had broken into the car one evening and used it as a love nest, leaving some of their belongings behind. At least, that is what my correspondent likes to think!

There used to be a house in Mirfield, now long demolished, which rejoiced in the unusual name of 'The Elbow'. During the 1920s a curious event occurred which was associated with a clock.

The youngest daughter of the family was lying in bed recovering from some childhood ailment, when her attention was caught by the loud ticking of a clock, except that there was no clock in the room. She looked across to the top of the staircase, which as in many of these old houses came directly into the room. The ticking grew louder, as if approaching the bedroom.

The frightened young girl now stared terrified at the stairs, the ticking grew louder and louder and then, as if from nowhere, a small man appeared. His features were indistinguishable, but on his head he wore a white hat, such as a plantation owner would wear, a white suit and white boots. In his hand he held what appeared to be a round clock which was ticking loudly. The figure, appearing not to notice the terrified girl, turned, showing the creases in the back of his jacket as he did so, and disappeared through the wall, at which the child screamed out for her mother.

Who the figure was and what the ticking clock signified, she was never able to discover and never saw the figure nor heard the ticking again. As the house is no longer standing, indeed the area itself has altered so much since those days, it has not been possible for the author to pursue the mystery further.

CHAPTER 10

Ghosts and Greasepaint

Many of the country's older theatres are haunted by ghosts more dramatic than anything which might have been acted out beneath the proscenium arch. The theatres of Yorkshire are no exception, although many managers seem reluctant to discuss the subject. Fortunately, the same cannot be said of touring actors and actresses.

It would seem reasonable to expect many of these ghosts to be of Thespians and this is certainly true of the ghost that haunts the Theatre Royal at Bradford.

The Theatre Royal is in fact haunted by the ghost of the legendary Sir Henry Irving, the son of a Somerset tradesman who, without doubt, became the best-loved actor of the Victorian theatre. After a performance of *Becket* he collapsed and died here on October 13th, 1905, but his ghost still walks the boards.

Another Theatre Royal, this time in St Leonards Place, York, opened in 1740 and was built on the site of the old St Leonards Hospital, founded by King Stephen in the twelfth century. As was the custom in the Middle Ages it was run by nuns. The theatre's ghost is that of a young nun who broke her vows and was walled up alive as a punishment. (As a point of interest, this explanation which is so common in accounts of this type of haunting, may be a distortion of the true facts. A spokesman for the Catholic Church told me that in the old days it was a fairly common practice for nuns to show their commitment to the religious life and rejection of worldly goods by having their cell doors bricked up, leaving only a small window through which they received food and drink.) Whatever the reason for this haunting, there are several people who are prepared to testify that a ghostly nun does tread the boards here, still wearing her grey and white habit. She is most often seen in a small room near the dress circle.

Many occupants of this room have said that they were aware of a strange feeling, as if they were being watched. Others experienced an inexplicable chilling sensation. The manager told me that strange happenings still occur and some time ago a well-known actress was standing in the back of the dress circle and saw the figure of a nun, dressed in grey with a white coif, leaning over the edge of the stage box.

But the best authenticated spectre at the theatre is that of an actor who died in a stage duelling accident during the last century. He was seen as recently as 1977, dressed in period costume and standing in the upper circle. He is said to wear a prominent ring with an awesomely large green stone and to have well-manicured hands. During the autumn of 1975 whilst rehearsals were in progress for *Dear Octopus*, the cast were assembled on stage to sing 'Kerry Dance Again'. They were puzzled to see a light slowly develop in the circle of the theatre. As they looked on fascinated, it increased in intensity and eventually took on the form of the head and shoulders of a man. This little incident only lasted for a few seconds, but it brought the rehearsal to a complete standstill until the cast had recovered their composure.

I have in front of me a photocopy of a letter sent to the *Daily Sketch* in 1965, from a Mr Harry Bennett of Hampstead, in which he says that while appearing at the Theatre Royal with his company, he managed to obtain permission to try to 'lay' the ghost. He says, 'Several of us occupied the dressing room and shortly we heard footsteps. The atmosphere became eerie and cold. To our absolute horror the figure of a tall woman appeared, hooded and gowned, having entered the dressing room through a closed door.'

Unfortunately, just at that time a female member of the company began to scream with fright and the apparition vanished.

The Palace Theatre, Halifax, was reputed to be haunted by the ghost of the comedian and playwright, Clarence Turner. 'Tubby' Turner, as he was known, collapsed and died on the stage in the early 1950s in the middle of his famous deckchair sketch. I have heard an unconfirmed story which relates how a local amateur dramatic society performed one of Turner's plays, *Summat For Nowt*, at the Palace. One young lady who had difficulty in remembering her lines, spotted a strange man in the wings, mouthing the words to her. She later learned that her description fitted that of Turner.

Another star who died on stage was the much loved character actor, Arthur Lucan, who together with his wife and partner, Kitty McShane, were a big draw at theatres and cinemas wherever they appeared throughout the north, as Old Mother Riley and her daughter Kitty.

Poor Arthur died on stage at the Tivoli, Hull, on May 17th, 1954, and I have it on good authority that his pathetic ghost has been seen on the site at least twice in the intervening years, dressed in his Old Mother Riley costume. Old Mother Riley was a great favourite with the kids of my generation, and Arthur Lucan's grave in the East Cemetery at Hull is nearly always covered with flowers, put there by children who never knew him but have seen his many films on television.

Alas, the Tivoli too has gone, closing down not many months after the death of Arthur Lucan. It was finally demolished in 1959 and a shop and office block was erected on the site.

The City Palace of Varieties in Leeds has had a chequered career. Like many music halls, it began life as the singing room of a public house, the White Swan, rebuilt in the 1790s on the site of a coaching inn. It was enlarged by Charles Thornton, best remembered for Thornton's Arcade in Briggate, to something like its present form and opened as 'Thornton's New Music Hall and Fashionable Lounge' on June 7th, 1865. The first chairman, in a long line of chairmen, was Harry Bowser, who wielded the gavel for many years before Leonard Sachs was born. It was closed in 1875 and was later bought by Mr Jack Stanfield and reopened as 'Stanfields Varieties' round about 1877. More alterations were carried out in the next couple of decades as a number of managers came and went.

Nowadays, of course, the famous City Varieties Theatre is better known as the location for the successful BBC television series 'The Good Old Days'. It is also a centre of mystery. There are several underground passages which are said to extend for miles – even as far as Kirkstall Abbey. Mystery also surrounds a coat of arms over the proscenium arch which, local legend says, was bestowed by King Edward VII, who is reputed to have visited the old theatre incognito to see Lily Langtry when she appeared there with Bransby Williams in 1898. He, as Prince of Wales, was staying as a guest at Harewood House. By tradition he used Box D, to the right of the stage.

The City Varieties Theatre boasts at least two ghosts to my knowledge. One is the ghost of a female vocalist and the other that of an old-time pianist. Who they are, no one can be sure, but at least one night watchman is on record as having seen them both on separate occasions.

The Georgian Theatre at Richmond is also reputed to be haunted, although the current manager, Mr Gregor Mac-Gregor, is unable to throw any light on it. He told me in February 1981, 'To the best of my knowledge there would appear to be no record or evidence of any psychic phenomena in the Georgian Theatre, although in its 193-year history it would appear that it should have acquired something of the kind.'

A letter to the *Stage* brought a response from Mr James Patrick of Salisbury who told me that when, in 1966, he took part in the Stewart Headlam Company production of the eighteenth-century version of *King Lear* at the Georgian Theatre, a lot of publicity was given to the sighting by the company stage manager of the theatre ghost. Mr Patrick went on to say that at that particular time there was a strong ghost tradition at the theatre, although he did not feel or see anything unusual.

As Mr MacGregor says, the theatre ought to be haunted. Samuel Butler first brought the theatre to the town in the days when Richmond was the fashionable centre of Georgian Swaledale. He was a theatre producer from York who found enough people in the area interested in the theatre to support his new venture and to pay to populate his stage with such people as Sarah Siddons and Edmund Kean. It became, for a time at least, the social hub of the Dales and must have been patronized by many celebrities of the Georgian scene. However, in time interest in the theatre waned and the doors eventually closed, the building being put to various other uses.

When rediscovered, it was a furniture store, until restored to its former glory under the watchful eye of Dr Southern, an eminent authority on Georgian buildings.

Thanks to the dedicated staff of the *Yorkshire Post* I was able to track down a record of the incident Mr Patrick

referred to and which was reported in the *Yorkshire Post* of
April 20th, 1966.

Mr Jock Evans, a London schoolteacher, was acting as
deputy stage manager for the Stewart Headlam Company,
during the production already mentioned. Working alone
in the theatre, he said everything suddenly went deathly
quiet and he became aware of a presence. After a moment
or two the feeling passed, the theatre appeared to come
back to life again and he returned to his work. The paper
reported that Mr Evans was not the first to have experienced the ghostliness, as other people had also felt it.

At that time, there were many who thought the presence
to be the ghost of none other than the great bard himself,
William Shakespeare, as the anniversary of his death occurred during the week of the play, and it was thought he
may have disapproved of the eighteenth-century additions
and subtractions in Tate's melodramatic and shortened
version of the great tragedy. It's a lovely thought.

Perhaps the reader will allow me, out of interest, to digress
here and mention two ghosts outside the borders of Yorkshire, but within easy reach.

A ghost has haunted the New Tyne Theatre at Newcastle
for well over ninety years: the shade of a stage hand, Bob
Crowther, who was killed whilst working there in 1887.
Ever since his death, many actors, staff and patrons have
experienced a strange and chilling presence and had the
odd glimpse of a strange man in grey, walking about back-
stage. A couple of years or so ago, a producer took the
advice of a psychic investigator, rather than have his company resign *en masse,* to try to put the spirit to rest. He was
advised to make the ghost welcome, by allotting him a
certain seat. Nowadays, to make sure that no one else takes
this particular place, a shrouded dummy is always left in
what has become known as Bob Crowther's seat, which is

way up in the gods. Where else!

The second ghost can be found barely a spit and a stride over the border, in the town of Ashton-Under-Lyne, at the Thameside Theatre. Here they have a ghost with the nickname of 'Ernie'. He always appears as a man in a raincoat, standing in the shadow of the upper balcony. The figure will beckon anyone fortunate enough to sight him, but once they begin to walk towards him he will vanish into thin air. Whose ghost this is, I have never been able to discover and the management seem rather reluctant to discuss it.

The audience has long since gone. The auditorium is empty. The safety curtain is down. The lights are dimmed and the players in some nearby public house celebrate their evening's triumph . . . or drown the despair of disaster.

Yet the theatre is still alive. Listen, you can hear it whispering in the corridors and stairways, watch its eyeless balconies gazing down, catch its breathing in the creaking of the scenery and rustling curtains . . . there is nothing more eerie, or more dramatic than an empty theatre.

It is not surprising that actors are far more respectful of the unknown world of the supernatural than any other group of people. For in many theatres throughout the land it would be ill-advised to tempt the ever-present ghosts to make an appearance.

CHAPTER 11

Dark, Mysterious Gentlemen

For every traditional grey or white lady in the county, there is a spectral male counterpart. The stories behind some of these ghosts may not be as romantic but they are equally as tragic in many instances. Some are doomed to haunt as a result of a foul deed committed in the course of some forgotten cause, while others, like the ghost of Marmaduke Buckle, are just there as a result of unhappiness.

Marmaduke Buckle was a crippled boy who lived with his family in a house in Goodramgate, York, in the seventeenth century. The house is still standing, complete with the ghost of young Marmaduke, opening doors, turning on the lights and, in general, making a nuisance of himself on the staircase. It is generally thought that Marmaduke hanged himself in 1715, when the torment of his disability became too much for him to bear. Scratched on the plaster in one of the upstairs rooms one can find the following words: 'Marmaduke Buckle 1697–1715'. Whether they were scratched in by the unfortunate young man or by someone else later, no one can really be sure.

Another sad ghost haunts Oakwell Hall, a lovely Tudor house at Birstall. A few days before Christmas 1684, the eldest son of the family, William Batt, was murdered while visiting relatives in London. The night he died, his family, knowing him to be in London until Christmas Eve, were surprised to see him enter the great hall and mount the stairs to the main bedroom, without saying a word to anyone.

They noticed how pale and ill he looked and on the stairs

saw a footprint in wet blood. Yet, when they looked in the bedroom they could find no trace of him. Not until the following day did they hear of his death and learn that he had been killed by a man called Graeme at Barnet. It's now believed that the ghost which roams the corridors of Oakwell Hall is that of William Batt.

As I write this chapter it is November 5th and I can hear children and their parents enjoying a huge bonfire in the fields behind my home. The periodic 'whoosh' of sky-rockets and the joyous 'oohs' and 'ah's' of parents and children alike, bring to mind a far happier and more care-free ghost which is said to haunt the lanes and footpaths of Nidderdale. This is the spectre of the young Guy Fawkes.

He has also been seen in the corridors of Scotton Old Hall, a place where he spent many of his teenage years with his mother and stepfather, after his own father died when Guy was only eight. Young Guy Fawkes was very happy here and his teenage years were spent doing pretty much as he pleased, riding, walking, and often visiting family friends, the Ingilbys of Ripley Castle.

It is a funny thing, but although we always associate Guy Fawkes with gun-powder, treason and plot, the spirit he has left behind at Scotton Old Hall, is that of a happy, aimless adolescent.

The ghost of William Constable haunts his old home, Burton Constable Hall, near Hull. This isn't surprising since in the mid-nineteenth century he did more than any other owner before him to turn the Elizabethan hall into a magnificent and comfortable home.

One night, a lady, sleeping in the Gold Room, awoke to see a figure in a velvet coat, standing at the foot of her bed. She recognized it from an oil painting kept at the hall as William Constable and was not in the least afraid, although she later claimed to have been more than a little startled when the figure allegedly spoke to her saying, 'I wished to see what you had done to my room!' Since that night, quite a lot of restoration work has been carried out at Burton Constable Hall, and where the ghost first materialized, workmen discovered a spiral staircase leading to the hall below.

Who is the silent, shadowy figure said to haunt the ruins of Scarborough Castle? Most people seem to agree that it is the ghost of a Gascon immigrant by the name of Piers Gaveston, late Earl of Cornwall and one-time friend of Edward II.

History tells us that it was here that Gaveston surrendered the castle to the barons about six hundred years ago, on condition that his life be spared to stand trial. Gaveston had become increasingly unpopular with both peasant and noble alike, but when the Earl of Warwick laid siege to Scarborough Castle, he resisted valiantly for quite a time before hunger and thirst finally forced the garrison to surrender.

Warwick promised both Gaveston and his men safe conduct but, once the gates were opened, he treacherously broke his word and had Gaveston beheaded outside the castle walls. (Many historians argue that Gaveston was, in fact, allowed to ride away, but that Warwick had second thoughts and sent some of his soldiers after him, capturing him as he made his way south and taking him to the town of Warwick, where he was then beheaded as a public enemy.) Whichever way it happened, Gaveston's spirit, unable to rest because of the treachery of his enemy, now prowls the castle ruins. A fearsome headless apparition, he rushes towards those who are unlucky or brave enough to walk amongst the ruins after dark, and tries to chase them over the edge of the battlements.

Walter Calverley, of Calverley Hall, nearly succeeded in killing off all his family in a fit of insane frenzy. These deeds give rise to the belief that if a group of people join hands in a circle around his grave at Calverley churchyard and sing:

Old Calverley, old Calverley, I'll have thee by thi'
ears,
I'll cut thi' into collops, unless tha' appears

then his spirit may be conjured up. Although why anyone should want to do so is beyond me, for Walter Calverley would revel in anything which had a touch of evil about it.

The Calverley family had been Lords of the Manor at Pudsey and Calverley for over five hundred years and, as the occupants of Calverley Hall, they were generally respected. However, every family has one and Walter was the degenerate of the seventeenth-century branch of the family; he drank and gambled to excess and invariably came face-to-face with financial ruin and all it entailed. Early in the 1600s, he turned on his long-suffering wife, a southerner, and accused her of being unfaithful. The more she protested her innocence, the graver his accusations became. Walter had, in fact, developed an unreasonable hatred towards the poor woman, just because she had been pleading with him to mend his miserable ways, even offering to sell her jewellery to help pay off his debts.

Now, Walter had a brother at university and one day a university friend came to Calverley Hall, to seek some kind of financial help. He couldn't have come at a worse time, for this was to send Walter into a mad frenzy. He stormed off into a gallery alone and set about considering his financial state, for this was his moment of great crisis. He ranted to himself about how his prodigal course in life had wronged his brother, abused his wife and undone his children, and the abject misery he would leave his children in should he die.

Suddenly, one of his children, aged four, ran into the gallery and Walter, now quite insane, slew the child with his dagger. Lifting up the bleeding body, he carried it into the presence of his wife and the second child. Then he stabbed his wife in the shoulder and killed the second child. Now of his children only his youngest son, Henry, remained alive, but being 'at nurse' he was staying at Norton. Walter set off on horseback, intent on murdering again, but the horse, driven too hard, fell and rolled on him. Before he could free himself and resume his journey, he was overpowered and taken to Wakefield, where his faithful wife actually forgave him.

Walter Calverley paid the price for his misdeeds on the York Tyburn, but not before the journey from Wakefield had been delayed for several months, due to the plague. He did not plead at his trial so his estates were not confiscated. His body was buried at St Mary's Churchyard, in Castlegate, York, but his remains were moved secretly to Calverley, where his ghost was usually seen at night, mounted on a headless horse. He has also been seen striding along a corridor at Calverley Hall, but I understand that this particular corridor has recently been bricked up.

His ghost continued to be active at the Hall for many years. A local vicar, when staying there, had his night's sleep disturbed three times after being thrown out of his bed by an invisible being.

The last mad outburst of old Walter was the ringing of the bell in the church tower, very early one morning. The bell tolled for a long time because no one could find the key to the tower. When it was eventually found, the bell stopped ringing.

It is a true saying that, 'The bad they did lived after them, the good more often interred with their bones.' As we have seen, it is certainly true of unpleasant Yorkshire ghosts. For instance, who was the saucy spectre who took a fancy to Sheila Broomhead?

Sheila lives in a ground-floor council flat in Cliff Street, Sheffield, and she was nodding off to sleep in September 1981, when the bed suddenly began to move from side to side. Then, something jumped on to the bed.

Now, Sheila may call an exorcist if the sexy spectre doesn't stop pestering her. She said, 'At first I thought the dog had jumped on the bed, but then I realized that was impossible, because she was locked outside in the hall.' She said that it was all over in a matter of a few seconds. She never saw anything or heard any noise whatsoever. It was all very spooky.

The Ingilbys of Ripley Castle were a proud family who produced one or two good ghosts in their time. One old Lord let his desires run away with him and although married had a mistress as well. He hid the latter, in the hope that his intensely jealous spouse would not find her, at Padside, a quiet spot between Pateley Bridge and Blubberhouses. Unfortunately the wife found out, tracked down her rival and cursed her husband, wishing him a quick death and an eternity of wandering in spectral form. Something he still does from time to time today.

A noisy ghost belonged to another black sheep, Thomas Preston of Low Hall, Appletreewick, about whom nobody has ever said a kind word. His spectre had terrorized Low Hall and Wharfedale for many years, making life intolerable with yells, bangs and groans. Eventually a priest had to be called to exorcize the noisy spirit, which he finally did by banishing it to a grave in Dibb Gill, in what is known today as Preston's Well.

Another ghost to be encountered around Appletreewick, haunted a lane outside the village for many years. At last a hardy soul met the ghost one night when returning from a night out with the boys. Made braver no doubt by the local ale, he approached the ghost and asked him why he haunted the lane, scaring the villagers. The spectre replied in sombre hollow tones, saying that he had committed an unforgivable sin and moved his neighbour's landmarks, one by one, shifting boulders and stoops until he had gained an extra strip of land. Disaster after disaster followed his wicked deed. The neighbour hadn't noticed but the man had been struck by remorse and had committed suicide by taking poison.

The villager listened politely to the grieving spectre and promised to do whatever he could to help. He promised to see that the stoops were moved back to the right place and agreed to pay back the chemist, to whom payment was still owed for the poison. At this, a weird smile crossed the face of the ghost, who faded into the night, never to be seen again.

Standing back from the main road and almost hidden by trees, is a well-preserved and beautiful old house, with stone mullions and a magnificent rose window above the main entrance. This is Lumb Hall, once the home of Charles Darwin. Today it is the home of 'Charlie', the resident phantom. He appears to be quite harmless and has the odd habit of making a shuffling and scraping sound at the front door. On investigation however, no one is ever found.

A few years ago, a lady staying at Lumb Hall underwent a strange and terrifying experience in the bedroom which she occupied. During the night she was awakened by an intense feeling of cold and was surprised to see a male figure in a fawn cloak rise from the floor and disappear through the ceiling. Some weeks later, part of an old staircase was discovered in the room above, evidently the stairs the ghost had known during its lifetime, the lower part of which had originally risen from the ground floor.

Lumb Hall is a large and interesting old house, with an equally interesting past. Within, there is a wealth of oak panelling, curious passages and an attractive staircase. The furniture is beautiful, having been made from period oak, which gives off an aura of olde worlde charm.

It has now been established that Charles Darwin, who was an ardent Royalist, lived here during the seventeenth century. Is he the 'Charlie' who scrapes and shuffles at the door? Or is he the figure seen wearing the fawn coat? Some historians believe the Hall to have been in the hands of Cromwell's troops during the Civil War, when the house was occupied by the Brookes family, ardent Royalists. Is this the ghost of one of the Brookeses? No one knows.

During renovations in 1949, workmen, stripping off old panels, found a number of swords dating from this period, which were evidently hidden away and presumably forgotten. Unfortunately, the weapons were regarded as just useless junk at the time and the unforgivable happened —they were thrown away. Perhaps this is why 'Charlie' is unable to settle and still wanders the Hall, seeking out his weapons.

During the 1920s, a psychic researcher spent a night at Bolling Hall, Bradford, hoping to spot one of the many spectres said to reside there, for apart from the mysterious manifestation the Earl of Newcastle was said to have seen back in 1643, mentioned in Chapter 2, the ghost of Richard Oastler is also seen here from time to time.

Richard Oastler, the self-styled 'factory king', was a regular visitor to the Walker family, who were resident here in the middle of the nineteenth century. He had threatened to haunt the place after his death if the Walkers' son did not change his mind and believe in life after death. On the morning of August 22nd, 1861, Richard Oastler died and his ghost was seen at exactly the same time, by the son of the house. It has been recorded several more times since, usually on the anniversary of Oastler's death. It is not recorded however, whether or not the psychic researcher was lucky enough to catch sight of him.

Hawkesworth Hall, near Guiseley, had a ghost of a Negro pageboy, who used to sneak into bedrooms and leave an imprint of his hand on the pillow. Also at Hawkesworth a cowled monk prowled through the corridors and galleries.

The Carnegie College at Leeds is host to the ghost of a former butler from the days before the building was taken over by the City of Leeds and was a manor house, known as 'The Grange'. He is said to have thrown himself off the top of the spiral staircase, when his love for his mistress was unrequited.

Jeeves would never have approved!

Ripon used to have an official called the Wakeman, whose job it was to protect the city at night. The last Wakeman was Hugh Ripley, who in 1604 became the first Lord Mayor. His old thirteenth-century house still stands in the market place.

By tradition, each evening a horn-blower blows a few blasts at the market cross and another blast or two outside the home of the current mayor. In the 1920s the mayor, who had married into the Precious family, who at one time had lived in the Wakeman's house, urged the corporation to buy it and preserve the building. He also suggested that the horn should be blown there as well as in the market square and outside the mayor's house. This was agreed to.

On the first occasion of the horn being blown outside the Wakeman's house, someone in the crowd shouted, 'Look up there at the top window!' As one, the crowd looked up and saw something white, with no distinguishable form, appear at the small window at the top of the house. Whatever the weird apparition, everyone in the square saw it.

People said that it was the ghost of old Hugh Ripley aroused by the sound of the horn outside his house. There were even those who were prepared to say that the ghost wore a smile at the honour bestowed on him by such a ceremony.

The Precious family lived at the house from about 1820 to 1910 and knew of the existence of a ghost. Many nights they had been awakened by a sense of some kind of presence in the room. Footsteps were heard, chairs which were in the way of the ghost as he walked the night hours, were pushed away with a clatter, and once a ghostly form was seen moving about in one of the bedrooms.

Many years ago, an old porter at the original Darlington railway station, which in those days was not much more than a country station on the Yorkshire – Durham border, had a frightening experience when, one cold winter's night, some time near midnight, he felt chilly and decided to go and get himself a hot drink and something to eat. There was a porter's cellar where a fire was kept going and a coal house connected to it. He went down the steps, took off his heavy overcoat and had just settled himself on the bench opposite the fire and turned up the gas lamp, when a strange man came out of the coal house followed by a big black retriever. As soon as he entered, the porter's eyes were on him and likewise the man's eyes were on the porter. They watched each other intently as the stranger moved over to the front of the fire. The stranger stood looking at the porter and a curious smile spread over his face.

All at once he struck out at the frightened porter, who had the impression he had hit him. The porter, quite naturally, struck back at the figure, but his fist went straight through him, striking the stone above the fireplace, scraping the skin from his knuckles. The figure appeared to stagger back into the fire and uttered a strange and unearthly scream.

Immediately the black dog seized the porter by the calf of the leg, causing immense pain. The strange figure recovered and motioned the dog away. Then, dog and figure backed slowly through the closed coal-house door. The frightened porter lit his lantern and nervously opened the door to the coal house and looked around inside, but there was no sight of either man or dog, nor was there any way in which they could have got out, except by the door itself.

Many weeks later, the porter discovered that, some years before, a man employed in the booking office had committed suicide by jumping in front of a passing express train. His body had been carried into the cellar prior to its removal. He had owned a black retriever, just like the one that had attacked the porter. He later said, 'I ought to add, that no mark or effect remained on the spot where I seemed to have been bitten by the dog!'

Another ghost associated with a railway station was reported by W.T. Stead in 1905.

The station stood just south of Middlesbrough on the old Middlesbrough–Whitby line. At the end of the platform stood what was known as 'the dead house', a small stone building often used as a temporary mortuary by the railway company, should any passenger expire on railway property. A young lad, by the name of Archer, was employed at the station as a telegraphist and, to him, the dead house seemed eerie and unpleasant. He was on night duty at the station and when he left his office in the early hours of the morning, he was always very uneasy when passing the building alone.

One morning, at about 2 o'clock, he came out on to the station platform and was walking in the direction of the dead house, steeling himself to pass it alone, when to his delight he saw, standing on the platform ahead of him, the familiar figure of one of the signalmen from the box just off the end of the platform. Hoping that he would walk with him past the dead house, he stepped up to the signalman but to his utter amazement and horror, the figure vanished as if into thin air.

Feeling very frightened, and not knowing what to make of it, he went down to the signal box and told the signalman on duty what he had seen. The signalman looked at him in amazement and said, 'You have just seen Fred Nicholson? . . . It's impossible. Didn't you know that he was killed yesterday by a train? His body is lying in the dead house at this moment.'

It was now young Archer's turn to be dismayed; he was perfectly sure in his own mind that he had seen the man . . . and yet the man was dead.

Finally, a much more recent and mundane sighting. Mrs Barbara Yates of Hull saw a rather interesting ghost not so long ago. She told me: 'I was fast asleep and was suddenly wakened by a rustling sound, rather as if someone was rustling paper, although I knew there was no paper anywhere in the room and certainly not near the bed.' Wide awake now, she looked up to see what she could only describe as a beautiful little boy, dressed in Edwardian clothes and the typical white collar which youngsters wore in those days. She said he had a lovely face and blond hair. The child smiled at her before fading away.

Mrs Yates saw the apparition on two other occasions,

each time standing beside the bed and smiling down at her.

Later she had another uncanny experience, quite unrelated, which occurred three weeks after the death of her brother-in-law. She said, 'One night I was unable to sleep, so I went downstairs without putting on the lights, so as not to disturb the rest of the family. I sat in the living room, and as I did so, my dead brother-in-law appeared and sat on the edge of the settee.' She told me she was not in the least frightened. The figure stayed there for a few moments, looking so real and unghostlike that Mrs Yates began to speak to him, which caused him to suddenly disappear, much to her disappointment.

CHAPTER 12

Some Classic, Authenticated Ghosts

There are a number of ghost stories, which do not seem to fit neatly into any particular category, but which are far too interesting to omit. Therefore, before we turn from the subject of ghosts and look at the other supernatural aspects of Yorkshire, perhaps they should be mentioned here. Most are very old authenticated accounts of hauntings, several of which have remained unexplained for many years, which to my mind, makes them all the more interesting.

To begin with I should like to describe one of the rarest cases of psychic phenomena that one will ever come across, the case of ghosts in law!

Only very occasionally has a ghost's evidence been accepted in a court of law. Records show that this did indeed happen in Yorkshire in the seventeenth century. The only case to gain notoriety happened in Scotland in 1750 and earned some celebrity from the fact that Sir Walter Scott edited the trial transcripts for the Bannatyre Club of Edinburgh, in 1830. The ghost in the Scottish trial was said to have influenced the jury, thus they found the prisoners in the case 'Not Guilty'. However, in the case of Rex *v* Barwick, heard at York Assizes, the ghost did just the opposite and Barwick paid with his life.

On April 14th, 1690, William Barwick of Cawood, pushed his pregnant wife, Mary, into a pond, holding her under the water until she drowned. Pulling the body out of the water, he buried it under some nearby bushes. He then walked to Rushworth and the home of his brother-in-law, a man by the name of Lofthouse, and told him that he had taken Mary to an uncle's home at Selby, where she was to be cared for until after the birth of their child.

A few days later, Lofthouse went to his well to draw some water and saw a woman sitting on a nearby hillock. He didn't take much notice of her but later when he returned for another pailful he saw the woman again, wearing 'on her cap something like a white bag hanging from it'. In his statement to the Assize at York in September 1690, Lofthouse said, 'Her face looked pale, her teeth in sight with no gums showing. Her looks being like my wife's sister, the wife of William Barwick.'

Lofthouse didn't tell his wife about the woman at first, but later, when he did finally tell her, she made him go to Selby and seek out the uncle to see if Mary was staying there or not. Discovering she was not, and never had been, Lofthouse went straight to the Lord Mayor of York and told him what he knew. Shortly afterwards Barwick was arrested and he at once confessed to killing Mary. Her remains were discovered where he had buried them and not surprisingly he was found guilty of murder. He was executed at York and his body hung from the gibbet. Documents held at York give details of the trial and of Lofthouse's evidence which, surprisingly enough, does not appear to have been ridiculed by Learned Counsel.

That story brings to mind a recent case, when a man was brought before a local magistrates' court for refusing to pay his rent, because his council-owned house had a ghost. Unfortunately for him, the magistrates ruled that ghosts could not be admitted to exist and, therefore, he could not refuse to pay rent on the grounds that his house was already tenanted. He lost his case.

In 1904, Mr E.D. Walker, a former mayor of Darlington,

told of an incident which had occurred when he was a child and living with his parents and younger brother in the village of Goldsborough, five miles north of Whitby. His father was a coastguard and was subsequently posted to Goldsborough in the 1860s. When the family reached the place, with all their belongings on the back of a cart, they found that there was no accommodation reserved for them. After staying at a local inn for several days while their furniture was stored in a barn, they were eventually able to rent the wing of a farmhouse, which had been unoccupied for several years.

They had not been in the house for more than three weeks, when one night the father came home some time between 12.30 and 1 a.m. He was sitting in the small kitchen and was about to make himself some supper, when the fender around the fireplace suddenly lifted up from the hearthstone three times and fell again with a loud bang. At the same time, one half of a double-doored closet opened three times and slammed shut with a crash. His wife, asleep in a downstairs bedroom, woke with a start and rushed to the kitchen to see what all the noise was about, only to find her husband sitting in bewilderment, trying to fathom out what was happening. They heard no more on that particular night.

A month or so later the coastguard's wife was in bed asleep, with her baby son in her arms, when she woke to feel the bed lift into the air three times and bang down again with a loud crashing sound. The poor woman screamed out in terror and lay, hardly daring to move, until her husband came home an hour or so later. While she was telling him of her ordeal, they both heard quite distinctly outside the window, what seemed to them like two dogs fighting in deadly combat, tearing each other to pieces. The coastguard took up his cutlass and dashed outside but discovered nothing. He now made up his mind to look into the house and its previous occupants more thoroughly.

The old widow who lived in the other part of the farmhouse, told him that previous tenants had moved out after only a short time, saying there was something wrong. But although she herself was only separated from them by a wall, she knew nothing of the odd happenings.

Two days later, a window cord snapped in the boy's bedroom and it was found necessary to call a joiner to repair it. He knew nothing of the house, but while working on the window, he was astonished to see a male figure draped in white appear as if from nowhere. The figure crossed the room and vanished. So did the joiner. He threw down his tools and rushed screaming in terror from the house. The coastguard dashed after him to see what was wrong and when he finally caught up with him, the breathless joiner explained what had happened, refusing to go back inside the house even for his tools.

About a year passed and the widow who occupied the remainder of the house died. The coastguard and his family were now in a position to buy the house in its entirety and set about having it modernized. (The Victorians spoilt a great deal of old property and furniture by their 'modernizations'!) One of the things they did, was to dig up the old flagstones in the kitchen and along with them the old hearthstone, and under this they discovered the reason for their haunting — a human skeleton.

Who the unfortunate victim was or how long he had lain there, it was not possible to discover, but once the skeleton had been given a decent Christian burial, the hauntings ceased and the family lived there happily for many years.

In 1979 I met a lovely old lady called Mrs Woodcock, who was ninety-three years of age and living in an old people's home in the West Riding. Alas, Mrs Woodcock died whilst this book was in preparation, but the story she told me is included here as a token of my respect.

She told me: 'My grandmother died in June 1880 at Driffield. Her death was a slow and painful one and a great blow to the family, especially my mother, who as the youngest of the family of eight, was particularly close to her.' The same month in which she died Mrs Woodcock's mother and father were married and went to live in Hull. In October of that year, her mother, who was now expecting her first child, was suddenly wakened by a feeling of someone kissing her full on the mouth. Thinking it was her husband, she sat up and was surprised to see her mother looking down at her and smiling as sweetly as she did in life. She was even more surprised when the apparition spoke to her and said, 'Time to get up, Sophia.' Mrs Woodcock continued: 'It was all so very natural, that it was a few seconds before my mother realized that my grandmother had been dead for four months. As soon as she had spoken those words, she turned to go into the bedroom which she would have used whenever she came to the house.'

Mrs Woodcock's mother sat up in bed and watched, as the apparition went out of the room. Through the open door, she saw her cross the landing, open the spare bedroom door and then close it behind her; all done so naturally and deliberately. She had on her nightgown and a wrap had been thrown over her shoulders, just as a mother would have done in those days when popping into her children's rooms in the early morning.

Mrs Woodcock said that when her mother herself died, she was living over a hundred miles away, but she was conscious of her presence with her; she felt as if she had taken her in her arms as she used to when she was a little girl and a feeling of irrepressible joy filled her heart.

There are so many instances of apparitions being recorded at, or after, the moment of a person's death, that they almost become tedious! They seem to crop up everywhere. One of the most famous and best authenticated cases of this kind which occurred in Yorkshire, is what has become known as the 'Birkbeck Ghost'.

In 1789, Mrs Birkbeck, wife of William Birkbeck, a banker living in Settle and a member of the Society of Friends, was taken ill and died at Cockermouth, whilst returning from a visit to relatives in Scotland. A journey she had undertaken alone, leaving her husband and three young children at Settle. Fortunately for us, the friends at whose home the death occurred, made notes of every circumstance attending Mrs Birkbeck's last hours, so that the accuracy of the several statements as to time, as well as place, was beyond doubt. Better still, this foiled any unconscious attempt to bring the statements into agreement with each other later.

One morning, just before eight o'clock, a relative, who was caring for the children while Mrs Birkbeck was away, went into their bedroom and found them all sitting up in bed chattering excitedly. The eldest daughter said, 'Mamma has been here. She said, "Come Esther".' Nothing could make the youngsters doubt the fact that their mother had come home, and the relative made a careful note of this fact, with the intention of mentioning it to Mrs Birkbeck on her return to Settle.

That same morning, unknown to the children, their mother lay dying at Cockermouth. It is recorded that she weakly told her friends, 'I should be ready to die, if I could but see my children.' She then closed her eyes, and her friends thought she had passed away. However, after about ten minutes of perfect stillness, she opened her eyes again, looked up brightly and said, 'I am ready now. I have been with my children.' She then passed peacefully away. The time — a few minutes before eight o'clock.

Apparently these events were investigated and subsequently reported in the *Proceedings of the Society for Psychical Research* and the notes taken both at Cockermouth and at Settle were in the possession of the Society for many years.

One of the problems with digging out old accounts of hauntings, particularly those written in the last century or the early part of this century, is that the writers very rarely give the name of the person they are discussing, when talking about ghosts. Regular readers on this subject will no doubt have discovered this and, like me, will find it annoying. One cannot help but wonder why Mr P—— of S—— Street, in the town of M—— was afraid to make himself known, or was it just that the author wished to spare the blushes of the townsfolk, yet at the same time, assure his readers that the person really existed?

Recently I was fortunate enough to come into possession of an account of an occurrence which took place in Middlesbrough in 1867. It is hand-written and dated 1879, but the writer has followed the annoying habit of calling his source, Mr R— of N— S— (North Shields?). Fortunately, he has told us that these events took place in Middlesbrough. The story is of interest because of similarities with that of the 'Birkbeck Ghost' and I make no apologies for reproducing it in its entirety:-

During the cholera epidemic in the north of England in 1867, Mr R—— of N—— S—— had an experience which had a great effect upon his boyish mind at the time. He lived in M—— St, Middlesbrough and was the favourite of his great-grandmother, with whom he often stayed. The old lady was rather a (recluse?) in her habits, and occupied two rooms in her daughter's home. She was known to have some (paper?(money about her, which, however, she carefully concealed from her relatives. At the same time, it was known she had a particular partiality for one certain cupboard which she used as a wardrobe in her bedroom. I mention these particulars as possibly explaining what follows.

At three o'clock one morning, while sleeping in his own home, Mr R—— awoke to find the old lady standing at the foot of his bed, calling to him and beckoning him to follow her. He sat up in bed, terrified at the sight, but of course, manifested no desire to move. The old lady became impatient, and saying that she could remain no longer, begged of him to be sure and go to 'the cupboard', this being her usual phrase when referring to the small wardrobe I have alluded to. On the old lady's departure, he was so frightened that he felt he (dare?) not stay in the room, and yet, strange to say, he had sufficient courage to get out of bed in the dark and hurry off to his mother's room, crossing a dark landing on the way. He awoke his mother and told her what had happened. She (calmed?) him as much as possible and saw him off to bed again, but in the morning was so much impressed by his story that she accompanied him to school, and they called to see if there was anything wrong with the old lady. Imagine their surprise on reaching the house to learn that she had been found dead in bed, but a short time before their visit. The body was cold (proving?) that she had been dead for some hours, the doctor declaring that she had died of cholera. The inference (formed?) was that she must have died about the hour she visited Mr R——. Suffice it to say, an inspection of the cupboard revealed the fact that other hands had done duty there before theirs had a chance, but with what result will never be known.

It is a moot question as to whether the apparition seen at death is the ghost of the person who has died, or whether it is the double of a living person on the point of death. Could it be that in most cases it *is* the double of the dying and not the ghost of the dead that is manifested to the living? These two cases seem to point in that direction.

The final story in this chapter is another one of Victorian origin, the story of a ghost which kept a promise made in life to appear to those dear to it. It was recorded in 1883. Many instances have been recorded since, but this one stands out as a minor classic amongst psychic investigators. Robert D'Onston recorded this as having happened to him personally.

The date was August 26th, 1867. The time, midnight. Robert D'Onston, then residing in Hull, had been for some time engaged to be married to a young North Country heiress, it being understood that on their marriage, he would take her name and stand as prospective Liberal candidate at the next General Election. However, for the sake of his bride-to-be, he had to finish an affair with a Hull girl called Louise. Louise was young, beautiful and devoted to D'Onston.

On the night of August 26th, they took their last walk together and a few minutes before midnight, paused on a wooden bridge running across a kind of canal, known in Hull as a 'drain'. They stood listening to the swirling of the water against the wooden piles and waited for the stroke of midnight, before Louise and he should part forever. In the few minutes before the clock struck, she quietly repeated Longfellow's 'Bridge', the words of which 'I stood on the bridge at midnight', seemed quite appropriate.

Midnight struck and with a final kiss the lovers made as if to part; but Louise said just before he pulled away from her, 'Grant me one last favour, the only one I will ever ask you on this earth. Promise to meet me here twelve months from tonight at this same hour.' D'Onston, thinking it would be bad for both of them to re-open partially healed wounds would not agree at first, but at last consented saying, 'Well, I will come if I am alive,' to which the girl replied, 'Say alive or dead!' D'Onston said, 'Very well then. We will meet, dead or alive!'

The following year, August 26th saw him at that very same spot a few minutes before midnight; and on the stroke of midnight, Louise arrived. By this time D'Onston, now married, had begun to regret the arrangement he had made, but considered it was 'of too solemn a nature to be put aside'. He therefore kept the appointment, but said that he did not care to renew their affair. Louise, however, persuaded him to agree to meet her one more time, twelve months hence and much against his will, D'Onston did so and again they left each other, repeating the same strange words, 'Dead or alive.'

1869 passed quickly enough, but in the first week in July, D'Onston was involved in a shooting accident. A party of four, including D'Onston, had hired the ten-ton yawl belonging to Thomas Piles of Hull, a fisherman and a reputed smuggler, to go yachting around the Yorkshire coast. For a reason I was unable to discover, on the fourth day out D'Onston was shot in the thigh by Piles and on the same afternoon, 1¼ ounces of No. 2 shot was cut from his leg by a doctor in a room at the Black Lion Hotel in Bridlington.

As soon as he was able to be moved, D'Onston was taken home again and is on record as having been treated by his own doctor, Dr Kelburne King of Hull. August 26th came and D'Onston was unable to walk without the aid of crutches and then only for a short distance, so he had to be wheeled about in an enormous Bath chair. The distance to the meeting place being quite lengthy and in view of his present situation, he felt he might have to disappoint the girl unless he obtained some assistance from an old retainer of the family into which he had married and who frequently carried out 'delicate' missions on his behalf. He also knew Louise.

Quietly D'Onston and his faithful retainer set out and arrived at the bridge about twenty minutes or so before the agreed time. It was a brilliant starlit night with a lovers' moon. Old Bob, the retainer, wheeled D'Onston to the bridge, helped him out of the Bath chair and gave him his crutches. D'Onston then walked shakily on to the bridge and stood, leaning his back against the top rail. He lit his pipe and had a comfortable smoke while he waited. He was annoyed at allowing himself to be persuaded to meet Louise a second time and determined to tell her that this was positively their last meeting. Besides, he didn't think it was fair to his wife. So, if anything, it was in a rather sulky frame of mind that he waited for his former lover. Just as the clock began to chime a quarter to midnight, D'Onston heard the distinct, click, click of the little brass heels that Louise always wore, sounding on the long flagged footpath which led for about 200 yards up to the bridge. As she got nearer, he could see her pass gas lamp after gas lamp in rapid succession, while the chimes of the large clock at Hull resounded across the still night air.

At last the footsteps sounded on the wooden bridge and he saw Louise pass under the lamp at the farthest end — the bridge was about twenty yards wide — and he stood under the lamp at his side and waited. When she got closer to him, D'Onston noticed that she wore neither cape nor hat and he thought that perhaps she had taken a cab to the farther end of the flagged footpath, and because it was a very warm night had left her wrap in the cab, coming the short distance in evening dress.

Click, click went the brass heels and she seemed about to pass D'Onston when, suddenly overcome with affection, he stretched out his arms to embrace her. She passed *through* them and as she looked at him he saw her lips move and form the words, 'Dead or alive.' He said, many years later, 'I even *heard* the words, but not with my outward ears, with something else, some other sense — what, I do not know. I felt startled, surprised, but not afraid, until a moment afterwards, when I felt but could not see, some other presence following her. I could feel, though I could not hear, the heavy clumsy thud of the feet following her; and my blood turned to ice!'

Recovering himself with some effort, D'Onston shouted out to old Bob, who was safely seated in the Bath chair in a nook, out of sight, 'Bob. Who passed you just now?' In an instant the old Yorkshireman was by his side. 'Ne'er a one passed me, Sir!' D'Onston replied that this was nonsense and that Louise had just passed him on the bridge. So she must have passed old Bob, because there was nowhere else she could go. The old man replied there was something uncanny going on. He heard her come on to the bridge and off it, but he was damned if she had passed him!

The following day, D'Onston, feeling unsettled, went to see members of Louise's family and was horrified to learn that she had died in Liverpool, three months before. Apparently she had been delirious for a few hours before her death and their parting compact evidently weighed on her mind, for she kept repeating, 'Dead or alive. Shall I be there?', to the utter bewilderment of her friends, who were, of course, unaware of her agreement with D'Onston.

CHAPTER 13

Fairies, Trolls and Spectral Hounds

I understand that there was, and for all I know might still be, a society in the south of England, founded in 1936 and called 'The Fairy Investigation Society'. It had over three hundred members who were pledged to spread the fairy faith, collect records of sightings and carry out research and field work into fairy phenomena. So devoted were they that when, in 1973, the Maplin Airport project was first mooted, they, like the conservationists and local residents, were worried, not because of the possible effects on the flora and fauna or on the environment, but because the fairies would have nowhere to go. For according to them, this part of Essex was a great place for observing fairies.

Many explanations have been put forward to account for the belief in fairies. Some chroniclers have said that a fairy is a special creation and exists in its own right. Others suggest that fairies, like ghosts, are the spirits of certain types of dead people, for example those who died before the dawn of Christianity or babies who were unbaptized at their death or were stillborn. Another popular tradition gives rise to the belief that fairies are fallen angels, not quite so wicked as to warrant going to Hell, but not quite good enough to be allowed to pass through the Pearly Gates either.

In many legends it is difficult to know where to draw the line between ghost and fairy. In fairyland, as in the land of the dead, the passage of time is miraculous and both fairies and the dead are said to haunt prehistoric burial grounds.

Are there really fairies at the bottom of the garden? Fairies have always inhabited the more remote parts of the

Yorkshire Dales, keeping well away from the marshy bogs and exposed areas, preferring the middle reaches of the valleys, where at a reasonable distance from farms and villages, they could dance until the first light of dawn showed on the horizon, to the sweet sound of the pipes.

The Craven fairies were often accused of kidnapping children and leaving one of their own fairy children in its place. But on the whole, Craven folk were on reasonably good terms with them, often entering into business transactions for fairy gold. Like the time a little grey man led his pony between the stalls of Keighley market. He was invisible to the crowd, unseen by all except one stallholder's wife. She was seen to leave the crowd, talking animatedly as if to herself, as she followed the invisible little man to the place where his wife lay in labour, for humans often acted as midwives to the fairy folk. Soon in the limestone caves near Settle, the stallholder's wife delivered a beautiful fairy baby, for which duty she received a bag of fairy gold.

At Burnsall, between Grassington and Bolton Bridge, the local drunk saw fairies dancing in the moonlight as he staggered home one night after a heavy session at the pub. For a while he kept a low profile, knowing it was unwise to disturb the fairies at play. However, in his excitement he forgot himself and called out, 'Nah then lads. Ah'll sing thi a song if tha likes.' Now the drunken renderings of 'Ilkla Moor Bah't 'at' at that late hour, was more than even the fairies were prepared to put up with and they set about him, kicking and pinching him. As he staggered away from the onslaught, he managed to catch one of the fairies and pop him into his jacket pocket, but unfortunately for the poor man, the fairy escaped and it took a lot of explaining to his sceptical wife, when she saw the state in which he arrived home.

A similar tale is told of how, some years ago, a farmer living at Kinsey was walking home over the fields one moonlit night, when he saw fairies dancing in the pasture. Being well versed in fairy lore and not wishing to disturb them, he skirted around the pasture quietly. The next day, returning to the field, he saw to his delight, hundreds of mushrooms, left, he was told, by the fairies as a gift for not disturbing their dance.

The fairies of Teesdale are more aquatic than their Craven cousins. Even today they are feared by Teesdale farm folk, for they demand a human life every year, usually through drowning in the Tees. Teesdale mothers still place knives in their babies' cots as a deterrent and it is claimed that by placing one's ear to the ground on Tower Hill at Middleton-on-Teesdale, the sound of fairies dancing to the accompaniment of pipes can be heard quite plainly. One Middleton woman claimed to have seen a fairy on this spot, with bright red eyes and a dress of green. Leck Fell has a pothole known as 'The Fairies' Workshop' where, if one listens quietly at the neck of the hole, the rumbling of the fairy lathes can be heard.

Perfectly sensible, rational people insist that they have encountered fairies at least once in their lives; and even in this century there have been some remarkable fairy reports, notably the case of the Cottingly Fairies.

31, Lynwood Terrace, Cottingly, was the home of the Wright family. Behind the house was a small glen where thirteen-year-old Elsie Wright liked to play with her South African cousin, ten-year-old Frances Griffiths. They also shared the glen with its tiny inhabitants, a number of fairies, which they set out to show to their sceptical family. Elsie asked her father if she could borrow the family camera and be shown how to operate it. For the sake of peace and quiet, her father agreed to loan it to her and showed her how it worked before loading it with film, expecting the resulting photographs to be bereft of fairies and thus close the subject and stop the girls' incessant chatter, once and for all. However, far from closing the subject, that first photograph taken early in 1917 was to set off a storm of controversy that still rages today.

When developed the negative showed Frances, posing with a band of dancing, winged figures, which the girls insisted were the little friends they had been playing with all spring and which Frances said were coloured in shades of green, mauve and lavender. They insisted they were the fairies that lived in the glen and denied that they had faked the photographs in any way.

A month later, the sceptical Mr and Mrs Wright were surprised when the girls produced another photograph, this time taken by Frances and slightly underexposed, showing a gnome with a pointed face, about to step lightly on to Elsie's hand. Elsie claimed he was dressed in a red jersey, scarlet cap and black trousers. The Wrights felt that somehow the girls had faked these photographs and they were put away.

They would have been forgotten, had not Mrs Wright attended a lecture on fairies at the local village hall, about three years later. As a result of doing so, she passed the photographs and negatives over to Edward Gardner, a psychic researcher.

At first Mr Gardner thought the photographs must have been faked, but experts said that they were genuine and showed movement of the fairy figures, consistent with single exposure. They could find no trace of studio work or re-touching and said that if they were fakes, they must have been done by a first-class photographer, and certainly not by two young girls. As always, other experts disagreed and said they were frauds, because since fairies don't exist, no camera could possibly take a picture of them.

As quite often happens in cases like this, the press, in this case the *Westminster Gazette,* sent the most cynical reporter they could find to Cottingly with instructions to track down the two girls and expose them. He retired baffled. Edward Gardner also went, with a loaded camera and marked plates and asked the girls to take more photographs with it in the glen. The girls obeyed, producing three photographs. One showed Frances with a leaping fairy captured in flight from the leaves of a bush. The fairy had hovered and then came so close to the girl's face, she drew her head back. Another showed a fairy offering Elsie a posy of tiny flowers. Elsie said her wings were shot with brilliant streaks of yellow. The plates were checked again after development and the most stringent examination of both photographers and photographs failed to support any other conclusion but that they were genuine.

Mr Gardner and Sir Arthur Conan Doyle published the pictures with an article in the *Strand Magazine* for the 1920 Christmas issue. Scores of people wrote in later to say that they too had seen fairies like those in the pictures. Sir Arthur called it 'an event so sensational as to mark an epoch in human thought.'

Not long after this, Elsie and her cousin separated and no more photographs were taken. They always maintained the photographs were genuine.

As recently as 1971 the photographs were re-examined by Mr Brian Coe, curator of the Kodak museum in London. He really put his life on the line by pronouncing them fakes, saying they were just cutout fairies on cardboard. Were they? Were they perhaps projected thought forms or are there perhaps fairies at the bottom of the garden after all?

If there are no fairies at the bottom of the garden, then what about the other, domestic form of fairy – the boggart, or as he is known in the Dales, the hob or hobgoblin?

The moorlands of the north east of the county are said to

be true hob country. Up at Glaisdale End, Hart Hall had a hob which would always turn up at harvest time and help in the hayfields, or with the corn threshing, often carrying on into the night, long after the farmer and his family had retired wearily to bed. One day, someone actually caught sight of the hob and noticed how worn and shabby its clothes were. It was agreed that a new suit of clothes be made and presented to the hob as thanks for his help around the farm. This was a mistake, however, for it is well known that hobs and witches cannot harm anyone until he or she has received a gift from that person. Still, the people at Hart Hall were lucky, as the hob only disappeared, never to return.

Similarly, the hob who lived at Close House near Skipton, threshed the corn and helped with the haymaking. He cleared off after being presented with a red hood. The owners of Sturfitt Hall, near Reeth, gave a hob a new suit of clothes and never saw it again, thus proving that this is the most effective way of getting the hob to leave.

A small cavern known as the 'Hob Hole', near Runswick Bay, is said to have been the home of one of these creatures. Local people believed the hob could cure their children of whooping cough or 't'kink cough' as it's known in Yorkshire. So, those children that were suffering from the malady were taken to the cave where the parents then sought the hob's help by reciting:

Hob-Hole Hob,
My bairne's getten t'kink cough,
Tak't off, Tak't off.

It was a hob, disguised as a beggar, which is said to have caused the disappearance of a once proud town. Beneath the lake at Seamer Water, there is said to be the remains of a town. Tradition has it that a beggar once asked for shelter there, but was turned away by everyone except a poor couple in a hillside cottage. The next morning the beggar had vanished and when the couple looked out of the doorway, they discovered that the town too had disappeared under the lake. It is said today that the rooftops of the town can sometimes be seen below the surface.

The many potholes and caves in Yorkshire are a natural haunt for hobs, boggarts and trolls, who often emerge at night to threaten mankind. There are tales of shepherds who claim to have seen little dwarf-like creatures, just before a storm, or at lambing time. Little creatures with bow-legs and hollow eyes, cautiously leaving their holes in the ground. One such creature lived in Hurtle Pot at Chapel-le-Dale, near Ingleton. He was said to have been responsible for drowning people in the pool at the bottom of the Pot; and a boggart living in Clayshaw Level at Nidderdale, was said to have pushed the wagons about. Trollers Gill, near Appletreewick, is the home of those shaggy-haired creatures, the trolls. A local story, recorded in 1881, tells how one man was riding near the gorge at midnight. His body was found by shepherds the following morning and marks were 'impressed on the dead man's breast, but they seemed not by mortal hand'. A similar accident befell a farmer who, returning from market under the influence, drove his horse towards Trollers Gill and fell into the chasm. It was whispered that the farmer had been lured by the trolls and had attempted the impossible feat of jumping across the Gill.

Kit Crewbucket is a female boggart who haunts the canal tunnels. She is reputed to have been seen quite often in Harcastle Tunnel, near Kidsgrove. Another female hob lived at Threshfield School at Linton-in-Craven. This boggart, called Pam, used to play in school during the night. Often the rector would write his sermon at the school and one Saturday he left his manuscript on the desk. Realizing what he had done, the rector returned to the school to pick it up. Pam resented the intrusion and beat the poor man about the head before bolting. The rector determined to rid the school of the tiresome hob. He knew that Pam was partial to a drop of strong drink and so one night he left a full bottle of brandy on the schoolmaster's desk. The hob became so drunk as to be incapable of moving, thus the rector was able to kill the inebriated imp and bury the body behind the school. Or so he thought. Whoever heard of anyone actually killing a boggart? Not long afterwards Pam returned, as mean and vicious as ever, to plague the poor rector for the rest of his life.

Not all boggarts take on a human form. What about those other denizens of the netherworld — the Hounds of Hell? Less pleasant than some of the phantoms one might meet in the houses of Yorkshire, these strange beasts roam by night, sometimes foretelling the death of a person they meet. It was a creature such as this that inspired Sir Arthur Conan Doyle to write *The Hound of the Baskervilles*.

These beasts are not exclusively British: similar 'Hell Hounds' abound throughout Europe and are linked either with stories that date back to the dogs of pagan Nature Gods or with the old Norse mythology of the 'Wolf of Hell', who is said to symbolize the death that springs from sin. Be that as it may, the mere thought of these animals was enough to terrify our ancestors. Branwell Brontë once wrote of them: 'The Gytrash is a spectre . . . mostly appears in the form of some animal — a black dog dragging a chain, a dusky calf, nay even a rolling stone.'

As I have said, the sighting of one of these dogs, hounds, Shuck, Gytrash, call them what you will, usually foretells misfortune or even death to the beholder, such as the black dog which is seen running and then falling from a ledge on the Corpse Way in Swaledale. A similar hound was reported at both Otley and on Ilkley Moor.

Kirkby Overblow, Cowling and Haworth also bring reports and on All Hallows' Eve in the countryside around Todmorden, where the reservoirs supply the industrial towns of the north, it is said the Hell Hounds rush across the water as easily as over the land, only to fade away as they approach the youth hostel at Mankinholes.

Appletreewick had a fearsome ghost dog with huge saucer eyes, shaggy hair and dragging a clanking chain. Flixton, on the A1039 west of Filey, goes one better and boasts of all things, a werewolf, equipped with abnormally large teeth which glow in the dark and exuding a terrible stench like rotting corpses. Its eyes are crimson and dart fire, while its tail is almost as long as its body. It is said to be capable of felling any nocturnal wayfarer it might meet.

History books tell us that in about AD 940, a hostel was built at the village of Flixton, specifically to shelter way-farers in winter time, from attacks from wolves. In those days, it was not uncommon for packs of wolves to roam these parts and they were regarded with a certain amount of loathing, because in times of very severe weather they scavenged the graveyards. Their cunning in discovering unprotected cattle, their boldness in attacking travellers plus their habit of suddenly descending in large numbers on an area where they had previously been unknown, all helped to give rise to the belief that the animals were not ordinary wolves, but human beings who adopted a wolf shape by night. A more modern theory is that at one time there could have been a member of the community who suffered from lycanthropy, a rare but real disease. The afflicted person behaves exactly like a wolf, even to the extent of moving about on all fours and gnawing raw meat. However, back to the wolves.

Their nocturnal visits and exploits were said to have been organized by an old wizard, whose innocent appearance enabled him to gather information about cattle, sheep and human wayfarers in taverns and market places. It wouldn't have needed much for travellers' tales of attacks by wolves to become distorted by repetition, and thus acquire some supernatural touches.

The Washburn Valley boasted a spectral dog that was able to hold a conversation in a broad Yorkshire accent. The story goes that, in the 1850s, a man living at Dob Park Lodge found a secret passage which led him to a brightly lit room. In the room he discovered a padlocked chest and a huge two-handed sword. On the lid of the chest was a glass containing a golden coloured liquid. The room itself was guarded by an enormous black mastiff, with eyes as big as saucers and bright as fire. As the man entered the room, the dog rose and said, 'Now tha's come lad, tha mun either sup yon cup, draw yon sword, or open yon kist.'

The man drank from the glass, at which the sword withdrew and the chest began to open of its own accord. A loud clap of thunder reverberated around the room and the dog set up an unearthly howl, that could be heard many miles away and all the candles blew out. There is no record of what the chest contained, but when the man eventually stumbled from the room and found his way back to the lodge, he was a gibbering idiot and his hair had turned snowy white!

At Kirkby Overblow, near Harrogate, a farmer left his dog guarding the sheep one bitterly cold winter's night and completely forgot about it. During the night the dog wandered back to the farmhouse and scratched at the door to be let into the warm kitchen. Unaware of the howling and scratching, the family slept on and the poor dog wandered off again and froze to death; not long after that, a phantom dog, which resembled the farmer's sheepdog, was reported to be roaming the district.

Not far from Whitby there stands a large old house, used today as a nursing home. Over 100 years ago, a girl was found dead in one of the bedrooms, having been murdered. Her black and white collie dog lay across her body, refusing to let anyone near her and refusing both food and drink. Eventually the dog died and the girl was allowed to be buried. Is this the dog which nowadays creeps into that bedroom each night, lying on top of the sleeping occupant?

Some years ago, a new member of staff was informed on being given the room, that a ghost had caused two nurses to leave. She laughed at this and said that she didn't believe in ghosts. She was to change her mind quite soon, for on two successive nights she woke up feeling as if she was suffocating. As though a large and heavy dog was lying across her chest.

In the late 1890s, a Wesleyan preacher was returning home after making a charitable collection in a rather lonely part of Wensleydale. As night fell, he found that his route led him through a wood, a mile wide. Knowing there was nowhere in the area that he could shelter for the night, he steeled himself and trusted the Almighty to protect him from the dangers of the sinister woods. As he approached the edge of the wood and found a pathway that would lead him through, a large black dog joined him and padded silently ahead of his horse. He could not make out where the animal had come from, but it never left him and when the wood grew so dark that he was unable to see it, he knew by instinct that it was still padding silently in front of his horse. When he emerged safely at the other side of the wood, the dog disappeared.

Just then, the preacher realized that he had lost his purse containing all the money he had collected. It must have fallen from his pocket as he made his way through the woods. So, turning his horse around, he set off back into the sinister woods to search for it. At the entrance to the wood, he was again joined by the strange black dog, which padded along beside him; it never touched him and he never spoke to it, but having found the purse he made his way to the edge of the wood again and as he emerged the dog ceased to be there.

Years later, two condemned prisoners in York Jail told the chaplain that they had intended to rob and murder a Wesleyan preacher on that night in the wood, but he had a large black dog with him and when they saw that, they felt that the preacher and the dog together would be too much for them. A useful ghostly apparition indeed.

Mrs Rita Dixon of Dewsbury had an interesting experience when in 1972, she was asked to take care of a friend's West Highland Terrier for about ten days, while her friends were on holiday in Switzerland.

'Two days after our friends left, Jamie, the dog, caught a kidney infection,' Mrs Dixon told me. 'We took him to the vet, who gave him injections and tablets, but that same night, the poor thing was so sick and looked so ill that we were worried he might not survive the night.' Mrs Dixon and her husband decided to take turns sitting up with the dog. She continued, 'I decided to stay up first while my husband went off to bed. After reading for a while, I noticed that Jamie had stopped being sick, but was rather fretful and needed comforting from time to time.'

By about 4.30 in the morning, she felt that the dog was settled enough for her to be able to leave him and try to get some sleep herself. Leaving him in his basket in the dining room, Mrs Dixon gave Jamie a fondle and then left, closing the door behind her as she went into the hall. She says, 'I made sure the door was fastened properly.' Then she climbed wearily into bed, making sure the bedroom door, too, was fastened, as the window was open and the door would keep banging otherwise. She knew that if the dog began to howl during the remainder of the night she would hear him, as since it was a fairly modern house the walls were not very thick.

A few hours later, Mrs Dixon woke up suddenly to find the dog licking her hand, which was outside the bedclothes. His tail was wagging, and he seemed more like the old Jamie she knew. She turned to wake her husband to tell him Jamie had come upstairs, but when she turned back, the dog was nowhere to be seen. Getting out of bed, Mrs Dixon went to go downstairs, pausing to wonder how the dog had got in, as the bedroom door was still closed. In the hall she also noticed there was no dog and the dining-room door was still fastened.

Opening it and going into the dining room, there was Jamie, tail wagging and making a great fuss. It was then she realized that her hand was still wet from the licking he had given her upstairs. She said, 'I wondered about the closed doors and thought back to when I saw Jamie in the bed-room licking my hand. He looked real. He felt real. I had fondled his ears and stroked his back and he had given me a really wet lick in return.'

Mrs Dixon is convinced that, although she didn't feel an unnatural presence, it was Jamie's earthly spirit that had visited her bedroom. The dog died a few years ago, but Mrs Dixon says she will never forget that particular experience and will never be able to explain it to her own satisfaction.

Finally, as a cat lover, I couldn't end this chapter without the mention of a phantom pussy cat or two. Cats, as we know, are supposed to be blessed with nine lives. But I am one of many people who think they may have a tenth. A great many people have been convinced they have seen the ghost of a cat. I think that both my wife and I have, and from all accounts they nearly all seem friendly.

Bella was a cat of this nature, a beautiful and well-marked ginger. Crossing a busy road near her home in Tadcaster, she was hit by a passing brewery wagon and died instantly. Some time later, her distressed owner was sitting quietly by the living-room fire sewing. She happened to look up and saw Bella basking in front of the warm fire, contentedly licking her paws. It all seemed so natural that it was a few seconds before she realized that Bella was dead and buried at the bottom of the garden!

Another pet cat was found dead beside the garage of the house, by an elderly lady living in an isolated house above Hebden Bridge. It was her well-loved black and white cat, Thomas. She and her husband had thought the world of Thomas and were naturally upset at his sudden demise. She called her husband, who gently wrapped him in cloth and, although it was beginning to snow quite hard, he took him into the garden and buried him under a small tree, where for hours at a time during the summer months the cat had used to sit or sleep.

One of his endearing habits had been to jump on to the window ledge beside the back door and, reaching out with his paw, rattle the door latch when he wanted to come in. A couple of evenings after the cat's death, the woman was alone in the house and was surprised to hear the latch rattling on the back door. On checking she was amazed to see it gently moving up and down — just as it used to when Thomas was alive. She told her husband about the incident when he returned home later that evening, but he didn't believe her, and said she was imagining things.

The same thing happened a few nights later and she told me that she thought it was her husband, who was not known for his sensitivity, playing a cruel trick on her. She told me, 'I had the last laugh though, for the next night we were both at home when the same thing happened again and my husband, too, saw the latch move. He dashed to the door and opened it, but there was no one there, except for the imprints of a cat's paws on the window sill in the fresh snow. No other prints were found, either on the step or on the path, just on the window sill.' Her husband, who has since died, never laughed at her again and she herself found consolation in the belief that pets, too, can live on after death.

A note of comfort for those who mourn the loss of a beloved and faithful pet perhaps? I hope so.

Although most phantom cats seem to be friendly, as a child Mrs E. Nelson of Cleethorpes had a real scare when her cat, Tiddles, returned from the dead.

She said that one night she was awakened by a loud purring and something pulling at her bedclothes. She sat up, thinking that her cat which had vanished several months before, had come home, but she was unable to find him, although she felt all over the bed. Thinking she had been dreaming, she lay down again and immediately the purring and clawing started again. Thoroughly frightened, she pulled the bedclothes over her head, but the cat, purring louder, pulled so fiercely at them that she had to hold on tight to the sheets.

She reported, 'I shouted for my mother, but she couldn't hear me, as I was under the bedclothes.' Shortly the cat stopped, but she was too afraid to look and just lay terrified until morning, waiting for her mother to wake up. When her mother finally did wake, the girl called her to come in as there was a cat in the bedroom. Her mother came running, but there was no cat, nor any way one could have got into the room. Nor were there any paw marks on the sheets.

CHAPTER 14

Yorkshire Witches

There are still several timber-framed houses in Yorkshire and Lancashire which preserve curiously carved beams that were once thought to be a defence against witches. The beams were planted upright to support the lintel over the hearth in the main room. A St Andrew's cross was usually inscribed at the top and horizontal bands were carved beneath it. Sometimes the date of the carving was added. Such was the superstition of the times, that it was believed a witch could not enter beyond the post; nor while it stood, could a spell be laid on the house or occupants.

Witchcraft in England was almost invariably a crime of the poor. According to trial records, most witches were old women who got very little out of their alleged pacts with the Prince of Darkness. In fact, the most they asked for was a roof over their heads and a full belly — not much in exchange for one's mortal soul. Still, this doesn't mean that all witches were innocent of at least attempting the crime for which they were charged, as many witches were convinced of their own powers and their ability to curse their victim.

The curse was the ultimate deterrent; always providing, of course, that the victim knew about it. Autosuggestion could, and still can, do a great deal of damage. Supposed proof of a witch's ability to hurt her enemies by supernatural means was produced at hundreds of trials. The making of clay and wax images was the common rite for inflicting sickness and death, and it was thought that whatever damage was inflicted upon the image would then be transferred to the intended victim.

Possibly the two most famous witches of all times, were Lancashire's Mother Demdike and Yorkshire's Ursula Southeil or Sontheil, also known as Mother Shipton. The latter was a grotesque woman who was destined to become our own Nostradamus.

She was born in July 1488, fifteen years before Nostradamus, to Agatha Southeil, a woman who herself had been tried and acquitted on a charge of witchcraft. She was born in a cave at Knaresborough, her mother dying while giving birth to her. It is recorded that Agatha's death was accompanied by strange and terrible noises.

Ursula was placed in the care of a local woman, who one day left the baby unattended in her cottage. When she returned with several neighbours, they were attacked by supernatural forces, finding themselves yoked by a floating staff from which one woman hung by her toes, whilst the others were compelled to dance in circles. When they tried to stop, they were pricked with a pin by an imp, in the form of a monkey. Ursula and her cradle were missing and later found to be suspended in the chimney, nine feet from the ground.

During her childhood mysterious events surrounded the cottage. Furniture moved up and down the stairs of its own accord and, at mealtimes, food would suddenly disappear from the table and the plates of startled guests.

In 1512, Ursula married one Toby Shipton of York and very soon showed an aptitude for prophecy which was to acquire her a national reputation. At first her prophecies concerned purely local affairs — whether or not someone would recover from an illness etc. — but soon they extended to natural and historical prophecy, often couched in subtle verse, one of the best known being:

'Carriages without horses shall go
And accidents fill the world with woe
Around the world thoughts shall fly

In the twinkling of an eye . . .
The world then to an end shall come
In eighteen hundred and eighty one.'

The verses go on to apparently predict such things as the Crimean War, the building of the Crystal Palace, steamships and the end of the world, although thankfully perhaps, she was off beam there.

Ursula was called Mother Shipton by the local people and, by virtue of her appearance, was well suited to play the role of a witch. It is said that she was of very big build, with a crooked body and frightening features, but that her understanding was extraordinary. She naturally aroused local curiosity and neighbours were forever prying into her private life. Mother Shipton got her own back by bewitching a breakfast party at which many of her nosey neighbours were present, causing them to suddenly break out into uncontrollable laughter before fleeing the house, pursued by a hideous imp.

They, in turn, informed the local magistrates who summoned Mother Shipton to appear before the court, where she is said to have told them that far worse things would follow, unless she was left alone. Then she shouted out, 'Updraxi, call Stygician Helluei!' and was carried off by a winged dragon, according to the magistrates' report.

Many of Mother Shipton's prophecies, such as the invention of radio, submarines, cars and metal ships etc., are now known to have been the work, not in the sixteenth century, but in the late 1820s of a man named Charles Hindley. Yet despite this, she still continues to be Yorkshire's most famous witch and the cave at Knaresborough remains as a memorial to her.

A ghostly drum which rises out of the waters of the well at Harpham and which is said to warn of impending doom, can be ascribed to the curse of a witch. The haunting of

Drummer's Well is connected with the St Quentin family, which was the most powerful family in the district and hereditary Lords of the Manor.

Legend tells us that William the Conqueror, after winning a nearby battle, promised Harpham and all the lands surrounding it, to the first person to reach the well from the battlefield. A drummer boy won the race, but one of the Norman knights, the greedy Sir Quintin, was close on his heels and he murdered the boy, before the others could catch up with them, throwing his body down the well. Unfortunately for Sir Quintin, the murder was witnessed by a local witch, who happened to be related to the boy and she put a spell on the St Quentin family, prophesying that the drummer boy's ghost would return to beat a death roll on his drum, whenever a member of that family was about to die. Which he still does to this day.

The ghost of an alleged witch haunts the A170, Sutton Bank to Helmsley road, where over the past few years a number of motorists have reported being stopped at night by a woman at the side of the road, apparently in need of a lift. However on pulling up, the motorists have been surprised at her sudden disappearance.

This is thought to be the wraithe of Abigail Glaister, mentioned in Edmund Bogg's *Vale of Mowbray*, published in 1904. Abigail was pursued by hounds late one night, during the reign of James I, because she was thought by many to be a witch. To escape the fearsome dogs, she jumped over Whitestone Cliffs into Lake Gormire and was drowned. According to Edmund Bogg, the ghost of Abigail was seen several times in the district soon after these events and a number of motorists in recent years have written to the *Darlington and Stockton Times* to say that they have been stopped near Sutton Bank by this ghost.

A skeleton preserved at the Leeds Medical School is said to be that of another well-known Yorkshire witch, Mary Bateman of Leeds, who made her living by skilful confidence tricks. The most famous of these was to show a hen, apparently laying a magic egg on which the words 'Christ is coming' were inscribed. In 1809, she was found guilty of poisoning Rebecca Perigo, one of her gullible clients, and was hanged at York and later gibbeted at Leeds.

It is said that souvenir hunters stripped the body and then the flesh from the bones, to be used as tokens of good luck, leaving the skeleton to be claimed by the medical school.

Near Hardshaw, in Wensleydale, there used to stand two cottages known as Rigg House and Rigg Cottage. Originally they comprised a single dwelling and local legend tells us that the division of the property took place for the specific purpose of laying the troublesome ghost of a witch.

Many years ago, the house was occupied by a man by the name of Metcalfe, a man of surly and forbidding temperament, who was disliked by everyone who came into contact with him. He had formerly been a slave owner in the West Indies and was known locally as the 'Black Whipper'. There lived with him for many years, an ugly old crone who was reputed to be a witch, who one day disappeared under mysterious circumstances. It was not long after that stories were told of her headless ghost appearing around her old home, scaring the daylights out of all who had the misfortune to come across her.

Metcalfe, much to everyone's relief, eventually left the area, perhaps because of the ghost, or perhaps because of the gossip and dark suspicion on the part of his neighbours. Where he went, no one knew or even cared, but the headless witch continued her haunting, much to the distress and fear of later occupants of the house. In time a subsequent owner hit on the idea of demolishing the central portion of the house where the ghost was usually seen, as a means of removing the unwanted guest. This action produced the desired effect and the ghost was seen no more, once the property was reduced to two smaller dwellings.

The ghost at Clapdale Hall, near Clapham, is thought to be that of one of Ireland's most famous witches, Alice Kyteller, who had the distinction of being the first woman in Ireland to be charged with witchcraft.

Dame Alice lived in Kilkenny in the fourteenth century, with her fourth husband Sir John le Poer, her first three husbands all having died under mysterious circumstances leaving her a great deal of money and the power and influence that goes with it. Arrogant and hard-hearted, she was generally disliked in the district and there were many rumours about her involvement in the Black Arts and Devil worship.

Things came to a head when her fourth husband began to suffer from a wasting disease and one of the servants told him of the rumours surrounding his wife, suggesting she may have put a curse on him. Later on going through her belongings, he discovered a magic talisman, a book of spells and other paraphernalia usually associated with witchcraft. Once they had a suspect, the church searched around for more members of Dame Alice's coven and many of her friends and servants were put on trial and imprisoned or executed.

Dame Alice, protected for a while by her noble birth and influence, eventually realized the game was up and that if she wanted to save her neck, she should make as speedy an exit from the country as was possible. She sought refuge with her stepson John at Clapham, where she lived until her death some years later and her ghost is glimpsed from time to time, aimlessly drifting through the rooms at Clapdale Hall, a victim of her own conscience.

It is said that Dame Alice had been so fond of her stepson that she was willing to sell her soul to the Devil for his sake, saying, 'I will do anything you ask to make sure the lad is always rich and prosperous.' The pact was duly sealed and Dame Alice was given a list of tasks she must perform, if the lad was not to lose his prosperity.

Every midnight, she was to be seen on the bridge near Clapham church, carrying nine newly killed red cocks. She would lay them in a circle which she defined with her stick. Then she stood in the centre and by waving her arms and brandishing her brush, she had to brush the water of the Wenning back into Clapdale. The young stepson's fortune never failed.

A man living at Broughton, in the North Riding, felt that he had had a spell cast on him, so he went to consult the local wise man, who asked him who it was he suspected of having cast the spell. The man said he thought there were two possible suspects, the witch Nancy Newgill and a poor village tinker, known to be possessed of the 'evil eye'. The wise man suggested that the only possible answer to his problem was to put a counter-spell on both the witch and the tinker. However, should one of them be innocent, it would recoil on the victim and thus further add to his sufferings; so he suggested the man should go and see them both and accuse them openly.

This he did, convincing himself almost at once that Nancy Newgill was innocent of this particular bit of chicanery. She looked at him, straight in the eye, swore a fearful oath and beat him about the head. The tinker, however, was so shifty-eyed and non-committal that the man felt quite sure that he was the culprit.

Just before dawn the following day, he and the wise man lit a fire and, while it was burning, they took a ball of clay, beat it flat by hammering it with the back of a bible, and then scooped out of it a rough figure in the shape of a man. Into this rough cast they next poured a vile mixture, consisting of pitch, boar's lard and bullock's blood; and the whole lot was then melted and stirred over the fire. What remained after filling the mould was divided into two parts and one part thrown into water, worked into a ball and thrown away. The other was thrown into the fire where it flared up into a bright blaze, throwing sparks in all directions. When this had died down, the ashes were taken and buried in the local churchyard.

The figure was then taken out of the mould and two holes inserted in it, to represent eyes. A pin was inserted into one of these, a charm incanted and the spell was complete.

As the man was returning to his home later that morning, the pain caused by the spell suddenly left him, and it is recorded that at the same moment the evil-eyed tinker was struck by a seizure, which caused him to go blind for the rest of his life!

Another well-known Yorkshire witch was Molly Cass, who lived for many years in Leeming Mill. One night the miller and three of his pals were playing cards at the mill, and eight times in succession one of the players, a man called George Winterfield, had the nine of hearts dealt to him. At the ninth deal, one of the group laid a wager of a guinea that Winterfield would not receive the nine of hearts again.

Just then, Molly Cass put her head round the door and told him to put his money back in his purse as it was not for Winterfield. The man was terrified of getting on the wrong side of Molly and he at once put his guinea back into his purse. Molly then said to Winterfield, 'Tha's gotten it again; tak' thi hand up and see!' The man looked and, sure enough, he had again been dealt the nine of hearts.

Molly continued, 'Tha's gotten it hard enough; tha's had it eight times already. T'Old un's in thee nah, and he'll not leave thi 'til he's gotten thi. T'Swale's waiting for thee, lad. Waiting to be thi bridal bed; the longer tha waits, the longer tha'll be astopping.' Winterfield turned white as he stood up, saying, 'I'll wed her, Molly. Give me another chance. Ah've rued all ah've done.' But Molly was adamant and Winterfield left the mill, saying he would go at once to wed his jilted sweetheart.

Now, whether he lost his way in the darkness, or whether there was a more sinister reason behind it, is not known, but his body and the body of his sweetheart were found the next day, floating side by side in the River Swale . . . The strange thing was, he had not seen the girl alive that day, for she had drowned herself several hours before he set out.

Just south of Blubberhouses, stands the small hamlet of Fewston, a scattering of farms, some of which were once part of prosperous family houses. Here too stands New Hall, the home of the Fairfax family, and it is from Edward Fairfax's *A Discourse on Witchcraft*, written in 1621, that we learn of evil doings towards members of his family, by local witches.

He tells of spells and black magic being used on his daughters Ellen, Ann and Elizabeth, by a group of local women believed to be witches, which caused the death of all three young girls. Edward Fairfax made allegations against them and they were brought to trial at York. Twice they came to court and on both occasions the women were acquitted through lack of suitable evidence. What exactly happened to convince such a man as this, that his neighbours were practising the evil arts and directing them towards his family?

According to the chronicles, the three Fairfax children became victims of the women, in whose company they spent much of their time. When Elizabeth Fairfax fell off a haystack and fatally injured herself, the blame was put on

Bess Foster. Margaret Waite was accused of taking a pennyworth of corn without paying, to use in making spells. Margaret Thorpe was accused of throwing pictures of the children into water, triumphant when they sank.

It is also said that several women had carried the three children to the fell top, to witness the Midsummer Eve bonfire, thereby forcing them to share in the old pagan feast of Beltane. When, a little later, Ann Fairfax died, this was attributed to witchcraft, and as we have seen, the women were hauled off to court, but were acquitted. On their release they returned to Fewston and celebrated their freedom with a celebration feast, to which they invited many of their friends and sympathizers. Dibb's wife, who provided the meal, was said to have been sitting at the foot of the table, while the Prince of Darkness himself sat at the head. It was said that the feast was so lavish, the food lasted right through until Good Friday.

Think of witches and one inevitably thinks of the Devil. Should the reader visit the churchyard at Kirkby Malham at midnight, you might find a banquet which has been specially prepared for you by the Devil himself.

The story goes that about 150 years ago, a boy and the vicar of Kirkby Malham were invited by the Devil to his banquet, which was all nicely laid out on a large family tombstone. The Devil said grace and chose a 'De Profundis', saying to the vicar, 'Don't you agree, my dear vicar, that a "De Profundis" is the most fitting, for a banquet of the dead?'

The vicar, who never could resist a good meal, agreed and looked greedily over the outspread feast. Reaching out for a delicious looking leg of mutton, he asked for salt, at which all the food — and the Devil — disappeared. So, the moral appears to be, if you do wish to take up the invitation to a midnight feast in the churchyard, remember not to ask for salt!

People believed that witches could turn themselves into any animal they wished, but the commonest one was the hare, possibly because it was an animal difficult to capture on account of its tremendous speed over the most difficult terrain.

A story is told of a woman who lived in North Craven who was suspected of being a witch and was subjected to a lot of gossip. The poor woman knew no peace. One day a group of men were out hunting when they saw a large hare sitting in the middle of a field. They gave chase and the animal bolted across the field, barely evading the huntsmen. Their dogs kept up with the horses, but one dog forged ahead of the rest of the party and as the hare jumped over a wall, the dog was able to snap at it and manage to bite out some of the fur.

However, the wall was too high for the dog to jump over and there the chase ended. One of the huntsmen who had witnessed the near miss rode up to the wall, thinking that perhaps the hare might still be in sight and possibly injured. He dismounted, climbed the wall, and there on the other side, squatting on her haunches, was an old woman rubbing her head from which a substantial clump of hair was missing!

Three rather merry revellers were returning from Boroughbridge races, late one crisp moonlit night, when they encountered a ghost on a white steed at the crossroads, just outside Norton. The phantom horseman pointed to a spot on the ground and then faded from view. Then, a stoat with a dead rabbit in its mouth crossed the road and stood in the place at which the phantom had pointed. Suddenly, an arrow from an unseen bow struck the stoat in the heart and at the same time, someone hiding in the undergrowth was heard to laugh out loudly. Each element of this macabre scene was to represent a future occurrence.

These strange events were blamed on a witch named Liza Horngill. One of the revellers, Owen Metcalfe, urged a crowd to drag Liza from her bed and duck her in the village pond. Liza screamed and cursed Metcalfe as, covered in slime, she crawled from the water, promising that two people in particular would be sorry. Because of the cruelty he had shown to Liza, Metcalfe's girlfriend, Alice, told him she would have nothing further to do with him and broke off their engagement.

That night, Gabriel's ratchets (barn owls) howled and cried, which was taken by the villagers to mean that someone had died. It was Metcalfe's ex-girlfriend, Alice. Her body was later found in the pond and it was accepted by all that she had been depressed about breaking off the engagement and had taken her own life.

Then someone remembered the ghostly happenings at the crossroads and demanded an explanation from Liza. She told him that the dead rabbit represented Alice, killed by the stoat before the crossroads were reached. The stoat died when the arrow pierced it and the arrow represented a stake. Liza said the villagers must tell Metcalfe to take the stake meant for Alice, who as a suicide would have it thrust through her heart, throw it into the air and catch it, three times.

Metcalfe thought it wise to do as was suggested, but as he caught the stake for the third time, a splinter lodged in his hand, causing some pain and in the end, tetanus. Before lockjaw set in, Metcalfe, in a deathbed confession, said that Alice had not committed suicide but that he had drowned her in the pond. Alice, then, was buried in consecrated ground; her place in a grave at the crossroads was taken by the body of Metcalfe. It was laid at the spot which the phantom horseman had indicated many nights before!

What about today? Is witchcraft still practised in twentieth-century Yorkshire? Many people believe so, although today's witchcraft is not so much magic as a serious form of religious worship.

The story of witchcraft and diabolism from ancient times to the present, is a long and often complicated one. Things were much more simple in the old days, when everyone knew that witches existed, had supernatural powers and could be fought in known and definite ways, by people with equal powers.

CHAPTER 15

Miscellaneous Legends

I have included in this final chapter some of the many Yorkshire legends which cannot be conveniently fitted in elsewhere. One could probably fill several volumes with such stories, but unfortunately, only a few can be recorded here. I have tried to provide the reader with a fair cross-section of legends, many of which turn up in other parts of the country in other guises, making it difficult for collectors of these tales to know where they really originated. For instance, this first example is a common tale in the British Isles, there is an Irish and Welsh version and other versions come from Lancashire, Lincolnshire and Shropshire. Tennyson even put a Scottish version to verse . . .

There was once a farmer by the name of George Gilbert-son, who discovered that his home had been taken over by a mischievous boggart, which caused a great deal of trouble and annoyance, particularly towards the children, who were tormented in a variety of ways. Sometimes their meals would be snatched from under their very noses, while they sat at the table; at other times the curtains of their beds would be shaken or a heavy weight would press on them, nearly causing asphyxiation. Their parents on hearing their cries had often rushed to their aid.

On the kitchen stairs there was a kind of cupboard, formed by a wooden partition in which a knot had been removed from one of the boards, leaving a small hole. One day, the farmer's youngest son stuck a shoe-horn into the hole while playing. It was thrown out again and hit him sharply on the side of the head. The boggart had been responsible, of course, but it soon became a popular sport of the children to put the shoe-horn into the hole and have it shot back at them.

In time, however, the boggart began to prove too much for the good farmer and his wife, so they decided to pack up their belongings and leave the house, letting the tiresome boggart have it all to himself. When the farmer was loading the last of his furniture on to the cart, a neighbour, John Marshall, came up and asked George why he was moving. George replied that he was forced to, as the boggart was making life intolerable. Scarcely had he finished, when a tiny voice chirped up, 'Aye, aye, Johnny lad, we're flittin' ye see.'

At this the farmer and his wife looked at each other and decided to offload the cart again, feeling that they may as well be tormented in their old house, as in another that might not be so convenient.

Wade was an imaginary being, connected with some monstrous tales of long ago, which were current for many years in and around Whitby.

Wade and his wife and son were said to possess the powers of the Titans, who could lift the hills and toss ponderous rocks. To their gigantic operations we should ascribe the castles at Pickering and Mulgrave, several Druid circles in the area and other works of prehistoric interest. In the building of Pickering and Mulgrave castles, Wade and his wife, Bell, divided their labours, a single giant being sufficient for the building of a mere castle. However, between them they only had one hammer, so it became necessary to throw it backwards and forwards between Pickering and Mulgrave, giving a shout each time it was thrown so that one or the other would be ready to catch it.

Young Wade, even as a baby, could throw a rock weighing several tons, over a vast distance. One day when his mother was milking her cow at Swarthouse, the child who had been left in his cradle on Sleights Moor, became impatient for his feed. He seized a stone weighing several hundredweight and, in a temper, threw it across the valley, hitting his mother with such force that it knocked her over. Her body made an impression on the stone which remained indelible, until a few years ago, when it was broken up for repairing the highway.

According to other versions of the legend, the old Roman road, known locally as 'Wade's Wife Causeway', was laid to accommodate her in crossing the moors to milk her cow. Wade did the paving and Bell brought the stones in her apron; once or twice the strings broke, leaving a large heap of stones on the spot.

It appears that the cow was as enormous as its owners and, many years ago, some practical joker tried to pass the jawbone of a whale for a rib of Bell Wade's cow. It was four feet long and four to five inches in diameter and for a number of years was on show at old Mulgrave castle. However when last seen many years ago, it was lying neglected in the joiner's shop nearby.

A tale is often told of how, not so very long ago, a little man from Guisborough walked into a shop in Whitby and came face-to-face with his own ghost. It has always been a known fact in the county, that this is an ill-omen, for to meet one's own 'doppelgänger' or 'waff' is regarded to be the sign of an early death. There is said to be only one path to safety and that is to walk up to it and address it boldly. The little man from Guisborough was well aware of this and without any hesitation whatsoever he called out, 'What's tha doing here? Tha's up to summat. Get thi sen home.' With this the doppelgänger slunk away abashed and the evil intent with which it came to Whitby was frustrated.

One of the best sources of legend in the county is my boyhood hero, Robin Hood. No chapter of this nature would be complete without one or two of the many legends surrounding him. When one considers it, so much has been written and sung about Robin Hood, yet so little is known. Where and when was he born? Was he noble or peasant? Did he even exist, or was he purely a legend dreamed up at a time of crisis in Tudor England?

Records show many people who could lay claim to the distinction of being this hero of countless ballads. There was Robert, Earl of Huntingdon, a dispossessed Earl who died in 1197 and who is hot favourite for the title. There was a Robert Hood who is named in various old documents who was disinherited in 1265. Other counties besides Yorkshire and Nottingham claim the man was associated with them. Lancastrians claim he was one of their sons, being in the service of Thomas, Earl of Lancaster, cousin of Edward II. Carlisle and even Scotland claim him as their own, adding that he used to cross the borders into the South, to help out in times of strife. (Mind you, we Yorkshiremen claim that Robert the Bruce was of Yorkshire extraction.) So, where do we look for the truth?

After reading through many ballads, stories and county histories, I have come up with my own theory that Robin Hood lived, not in the reign of King Richard, but in the reign of Edward II, and he was indeed a 'Tyke'.

I believe he was Robert Hood, who was *valet de chambre* at Edward II's court, who was born in Wakefield and following defection during the Royal Progress through Lancashire, was outlawed. He took to the open-air life, after disappearing into the Don Valley. Here he met a forester and in answer to the forester's challenge, swore to kill him, after telling him he was 'Robin Hood, a Yorkshire outlaw'.

Sir Guy of Gisburn, we learn, was not at all what he

seemed to be from the ballads such as *The Geste of Robyn Hode* (1550), or the 16th Century *Lyfe of Robyn Hode*. He was in fact a forester of Gisburn, an area between Pendle and the Forest of Bowland, who swore to rid his forest of the arrogant waster. So, we now have the beginnings of a saga which was to develop over the next few centuries. In time troops were sent to arrest Robert Hood and, according to Lionel Charlton, in his *History of Whitby* published in 1779, Robert Hood retired northwards across the moors that surround Whitby, where gaining the sea coast, he took up with a group of fishermen, even trying his hand at piracy. In time, he either became fed up with the life of a fisherman or, more likely, was chased out of Whitby for stealing, and he again took up the life of an outlaw in the greenwood.

As time went on the story took on extra characters, all of whom were invented by minstrels. The foremost characters being Little John, Friar Tuck, Much the miller's son, Alan a'Dale and Will Scarlet. Next the ballad writers decided to add a little sex to the saga, by inventing Maid Marion, who was probably adapted from the Queen of the May traditions.

The period of Robin Hood covered times of acute disturbance, when many good Englishmen were driven to living outside the law, where they preyed on wealthy merchants, barons and abbey agents, except that they did it for themselves and not to give to the poor.

Robert Hood was most probably killed in a brawl, but legend has him dying at Kirklees Priory, near Wakefield. Let me, if I may, quote from a very old manuscript I was recently shown by a writer engaged in research into Robin Hood:

The Cistercian Priory of Kirklees was one of the lesser monasteries . . . Elizabeth Stainton is said to have been its first Prioress but this is very doubtful, although she may have been a relative of the Robert Hood mentioned in the ballads . . . The most perfect relic now remaining of the Priory is a house usually called the Gatehouse. A room in this building is said to have been the scene of Robin Hood's death and the supposed grave of the outlaw lies on rising ground, some distance from the gatehouse, from the window of which he is said to have shot his last arrow.

All very romantic, but is it true? It is believed that Robin Hood, when an old man, lived in retirement for some time outside the Priory and that the Prioress was responsible for his death through over-bleeding him, in an effort to rid him of his fever. He is said to have been able to blow three weak blasts on his hunting horn to summon the faithful Little John, who was too late to do anything other than carry out Robin's last request. He helped him string his bow, supported him at his cell window, and where the arrow fell, there our hero was to be buried. Genuine or not, the grave at Kirklees has been visited by thousands over the centuries and many believe this is where bold Robin is lying.

Of the stone which covered the grave, only a fragment now remains, encircled in an iron cage to prevent further damage, for in days gone by, chips of stone were carried away, not as mementos, but, would you believe, as a cure for toothache.

Hear undernead dis laith stean
Laiz robert earl of Huntingtun
Near arcir ver az hie sa geud
An pipl kauld im robin heud
Sick utlawz az in an iz men
Vil england nivr si agen.

                    obiit 24 kal dekembris 1247.

Here, under this little stone,
Lies Robert, Earl of Huntingdon.
Ne'er archer was as him so good,
And people called him Robin Hood.
Such outlaws as he and his men
Will England never see again.

Died December 24th, 1247.

So ran the inscription on his alleged gravestone at Kirklees Priory.

Like all true Yorkshiremen, I am a brass band fanatic and my own favourite Yorkshire legend concerns a village brass band.

A certain colliery village in South Yorkshire had a very good and enthusiastic band, renowned not only throughout Yorkshire, but throughout the neighbouring counties, for the quality and excellence of its music. One year, many years ago, they reached the grand finals of the National Brass Band Championships at Belle Vue, Manchester.

For weeks they practised their pieces until they were note perfect. For days before the event, the instruments were polished until they shone like glass. The uniforms were brushed and pressed until in the end they would have done credit to any regimental bandmaster. Came the great day and they clambered aboard one of Camplejohn Brother's coaches amidst vociferous good wishes from their many supporters and set out for the finals where, to the delight of everyone, they took first place.

After the event there followed the usual liquid refreshments so that by the time they arrived back at the village it was well past midnight and most of the inhabitants had long since retired to their beds. Not wishing to wake them, the bandsmen took off their boots before alighting from the coach, so that as they marched in proper military fashion, befitting such an august occasion, their stockinged feet would make no noise on the cobbled streets – but they couldn't help marching to the rousing refrain of 'See The Conquering Heroes Come!'

That same year, the band were asked to play carols around the Christmas tree in Doncaster market, on the last Saturday before Christmas. A local vicar led the prayers and the hymn singing, which got under way with 'Christians Awake'. Just as they reached the final verse, a bull broke out of one of the stockades and, head down, charged straight for the band, who led by the vicar, headed for the nearest refuge. This happened to be a narrow doorway which led up a flight of stairs to a room belonging to the local St John's Ambulance Brigade.

All the bandsmen, including the vicar, managed to crowd onto the narrow stairs, all that is, except the bass drummer, who was left struggling in the doorway, his drum wedged half in and half out of the door. The bull stood silently pawing the ground for a second or two, ready to charge the poor struggling man. The vicar, seeing what was about to happen, called from his place of safety at the top of the stairs, 'Trust in the Lord, brothers.' To which the panic-stricken bass drummer replied, 'Never mind him. Trust in this bloody drum. If this gives way we've all bloody well had it!' . . . Or words to that effect.

I don't suppose that Bowes, since the desecration of the boundaries, can be called a part of Yorkshire anymore. But as most Yorkshirefolk don't recognize the new borders anyway, for the purposes of this book they don't exist.

A strange legend exists which concerns the desertion by the Roman Legion of their fort at Bowes. The soldiers were recalled to Rome, and their disregard for discipline led to the wholesale pillaging of the garrison by local peasants who invaded it and slaughtered every last Roman. They were too late if they expected to find any loot, for the Roman soldiers had secretly buried it, evidently hoping to retrieve it at a later date. So, although the locals searched high and low, they found not a trace of the gold and valuables they had intended to steal.

For many years the place was shunned, particularly after dark and especially on the anniversary of the massacre, for each year on that date the ghosts of the slain Roman soldiers appeared, busily engaged in burying gold and valuables. Local tradition says that in the sixteenth century, two local men hid inside the ruins of the fort on the night of the anniversary. The following day they told a fantastic story of a procession of soldiers carrying a huge chest of gold, which they then buried. But still the treasure has never been found, for before the men could tell of its whereabouts, they both met with violent deaths within hours of each other.

The first was slain by his friend, who then grovelled in the earth for the chest. A blood-red hand appeared, led the murderer over the body of his friend and dragged him screaming, across the fields to the bank of the Greta, where his body was found the next day.

Swaledale people proudly boast that their regional capital, Richmond, is the most beautiful town in England. There are many legends about knights, ghosts and treasure connected with Richmond Castle, which even though a ruin is an imposing sight as it rises majestically above the River Swale. About a mile away from the castle stands the remains of Easby Abbey and, between the two, phantom drumming has been heard rising from the ground. It is the echo of a tragedy that is said to have befallen a drummer boy, who was stationed at the castle many years ago.

Early in the last century, a tunnel was discovered behind the inner walls of the castle, by a potter called Thompson, or Thomas. He is reported to have followed the passage, which took him down beneath the keep and into the hillside, where it ended in a chamber. Here an amazing sight met his eyes, for he found King Arthur and his knights asleep. On a big round table rested a horn and sword, but as he went to pick them up, one of the knights stirred and opened his eyes. The terrified potter dropped the sword and the horn and fled in sheer terror. Ever after he refused to identify the tunnel he had followed and despite many attempts by others, the tunnel remained undiscovered for many years.

It would probably have been forgotten had a soldier from the garrison not stumbled on the entrance, when a paving stone collapsed. The entrance was too small for him to squeeze into, so a drummer boy was summoned and thrust through the entrance, after being told to beat his drum as he walked, so that his movements could be followed on the surface. Unfortunately the exercise ended in tragedy. The drum-beats faded slowly until they were heard no more and the poor little drummer boy was lost forever.

Whenever we talk of buried treasure, we nearly always think of pirates, the Spanish Main and exotic tropical islands. Yorkshire might not be what one could call exotic, but if the legends are to be believed, there is plenty of treasure buried here, just lying around waiting to be discovered. Every period of unrest, from the Romans and Vikings to the Civil War, has produced its crop of legends and perhaps one of the most interesting comes from the Reformation period, when church plate and ornaments are reputed to have been hidden away in vast quantities to avoid the greedy hands of the blacksmith's son-cum-chief advisor to Henry VIII, Thomas Cromwell and the King's Commissioners.

During this period, one Henry Pearson, treasurer of

Kirkstall Abbey, is said to have hidden away the abbey valuables. Some people say they consisted of church plate and chalices, while others think the treasure was more likely to consist of hoards of gold and silver plate. Stories concerning the Kirkstall Abbey treasures have been handed down through the centuries, but as yet no trace has ever been found.

Stamford Bridge is also said to be a paradise for treasure hunters, for here, near the site of the old bridge, is where Harold fought the Norwegians under Hadrada and Tostig, some nine hundred years ago. There is a real possibility that the booty taken by the victors after the battle never left the field and has been hidden beneath the mud ever since.

As every schoolboy knows, the Battle of Stamford Bridge was fought in a bit of a hurry. Harold was on the south coast waiting to do battle with the Normans, who were preparing an invasion, when news reached him that the upstart Norwegians were raping and pillaging in the north. By the time Harold and his army reached York, the city was already in ruins and the Norwegians, laden down with loot, had got as far as Stamford. There Harold engaged them and after a ferocious battle, which lasted all day, gained a decisive victory. The booty taken was tremendous: plate from the abbeys and monasteries, loot from the great houses which lay in their path, jewels and gold from the treasury at York. Hardly had the victorious Saxon army gathered it up, when the news arrived that the Normans had landed at Hastings.

Harold was in a hurry to get to grips with the Normans and instructed his men to march south with all speed, travelling light. Therefore the treasure had to be hidden before the march began, a march they accomplished in record time. The outcome of the Battle of Hastings is well known and few Saxons survived to return to Stamford to retrieve the hoards buried there. Today, untold wealth is believed to lie beneath the meadows and the feet of the many anglers who fish this popular spot.

One character we haven't discussed in this chapter so far, is the Old Lad himself. The Devil plays quite a large role in local legends throughout Great Britain, especially in connection with unusual formations of earth and stone — earthworks; ancient tombs and barrows; megaliths and even natural boulders which, because of their isolated position have, after centuries of erosion by wind and rain, taken on a particularly striking shape.

For instance, at Boroughbridge there are three such stones, each one being between eighteen and twenty feet high, known as the 'Devil's Arrows', running in line north to south. Legend tells us that the Devil destroyed Aldborough after taking his stand on Howe Hill and hurling the huge stones at the town. These monoliths are said to be some of the missiles which he left sticking out of the ground. I don't think he particularly liked the people of Yorkshire, for he is said to have done the same to the people of Hartforth, flinging a huge mass of stone at them from Gilling, some distance away, and shouting as he hurled it:

'Have 'at thee, black Hartforth,
But have a care o' bonny Gilling.'

The rock, which bears the Devil's fingerprints, can still be found on Gatherley Moor.

The Domesday Book mentions a large stone, about twenty feet in height, which can be found in the churchyard at Rudston. Here again, local legend tells us that it was thrown by the Devil at workmen who were building the church. He is also held responsible for the building of Filey Brigg, a dangerous reef, for the express purpose of endangering sailors. Local fishermen will tell you that while he was busy with this feat, he dropped his hammer into the North Sea and dived into the water to retrieve it. Fumbling about in the murky depths, he seized a haddock, thinking it was his hammer handle, and the dark marks seen on this particular fish are again said to be an impression of the Devil's fingers. (Another legend associated with these marks, attributes them to the fingers of St Peter, this of course being the fish he caught, which was found to have the tribute money in its mouth.)

There is a legend that the bridge over the border at Kirkby Lonsdale was built by the Devil and that his apron strings broke as he was carrying stones for the building work, throwing the boulders into the river. There is a 'Devil's Apronful' on Pockstones Moor, near Appletreewick, said to have been left there when he was filling up the ghill. There is also the 'Great Apronful' and the 'Little Apronful' near the Cow and Calf Rocks, on Ilkley Moor, which have a similar legend behind them.

Another bridge associated with him, is Kilgrim Bridge, up in North Yorkshire. The story behind this bridge is that on completion of his handiwork, the Devil demanded the first living thing which crossed it. The locals, when it was completed, threw a loaf of bread on to it and Grim, a shepherd's dog, ran after it, thus becoming the sacrifice and giving his name to the bridge.

Of course, trying to outwit the Devil was an art in itself. Many are said to have succeeded, for example the licentious monk from Rievaulx Abbey. He loved good living and loose women and the Devil, always on the lookout for the unwary, promised him all the best food and wine and the most beautiful women in the county for the rest of his natural life, providing he signed the usual bond giving him his soul, twenty years hence. The wily monk consented, providing he could insert one stipulation after the bond was signed. The Devil agreed and when the document was completed, he asked what the stipulation was. The monk said, 'That you shall find me a virgin and an honest man in Pickering!' The Devil set out to perform this task, which he found impossible. He ranted and raged for days, causing hail, thunder and lightning to strike the abbey, but it was to no avail and the Devil had to concede defeat at the hands of the wily old monk.

Sometimes, for a change, the Devil would appear in different guises, and one of his favourites was as a serpent or worm. It was in this guise that he appeared in a cave at Slingsby, on the B 1257, north west of Malton. His body was said to have been a mile long and he ravaged the countryside for many months, before one Marmaduke Wyvil of Slingsby destroyed him with the aid of his dog. The incident is remembered by a monument to man and dog, which can be found in Osgodby Church. The Devil also turned up as a serpent at Lofthouse where there is an upright stone, traditionally said to mark the site of his lair. Here again he was defeated by a mere human, a man by the name of Scaw.

THE END?

Well not quite . . . for the ghosts of Yorkshire's past will
always be with us.
Tomorrow — today will become yesterday.
And today is the birthday of tomorrow's
ghosts.
(If you see what I mean)

Terence W. Whitaker.

Index